AMERICA'S POLITICAL COLD WAR

Conservatives vs. Liberals

Why Neither Side Can Win

Don Durrett

(Third Edition, July 2022)

Copyright © 2022 by Donald David Durrett
All rights reserved.

ISBN: 979-8-218-00990-8

www.DONDURRETT.com

BOOKS BY DON DURRETT

The Path Forward

A Stranger From the Past

Conversations With an Immortal

Finding Your Soul

The Way

New Thinking for the New Age

Spirit Club

Last of the Gnostics

The Gathering

Ascension Training

Team Creator

Get Healthy, Stay Healthy

Post America: A New Constitution

The Demise of America

Kern County: The Path to Secession and a New Constitution

Without freedom of thought, there can be no such thing as wisdom. And no such thing as liberty, without freedom of speech.

– Benjamin Franklin.

Democracy and freedom are not compatible. Thereby, freedom must be defined in the Constitution. Otherwise, freedom will be lost.

 – Author's viewpoint.

There is only one consciousness, which we all share. Thus, separation is a lie.

 – The Guides.

Contents

Introduction 1

Chapter One
The Political Cold War 5

Chapter Two
The Two Parties 19

Chapter Three
Their Narratives 35

Chapter Four
Trump & Sanders 53

Chapter Five
MMT and Economics 65

Chapter Six
Free Speech 77

Chapter Seven
Collectivism vs. Individualism 89

Chapter Eight
The Path Forward 99

Conclusion
Some Added Thoughts 109

Appendix One
A New Constitution 115

Appendix Two
Michael teachings 139

Introduction

The first thing I need to do is define the two warring parties in this political cold war. I'm going to use the term "conservative" to designate the warring Republicans. These are Republicans that you would consider to be far-right loyalists. They consider RINOs (Republicans in name only) to be apostate Republicans. They are not moderate in their beliefs, but mostly see issues from a rigid Republican viewpoint and toe the line in what Republicans hold sacred.

So, when I use the term "conservative," this is the group that I am referring to.

Their warring opponent is easy to guess. These are progressive liberal socialists. These are the far-left liberals. I'm going to use the term "liberal" to designate them in this book to make it easier to read. Note that I am not referring to moderate liberals, who are not aligned with many progressive socialist ideas and agendas.

So, when I use the term "liberal," I'm referring to far-left liberals who agree with the progressive socialist agenda that is currently in vogue with many in the Democratic Party. I will use the term "leftist-socialist" on occasion for clarity to identify this new American political movement.

This book is highly controversial. I'm definitely over the target. The two warring parties in this political cold war (the liberals and the conservatives) don't want to talk about it. They want to pretend that it does not exist. Well, I'm going to expose them and reveal that it does exist. Both sides will hate this book. It's really a lose-lose situation for me.

Why do I want to get in the middle of a war with both sides angry at me? Why? Because I have an agenda. First, to inform you that this war is occurring and explain why there will be no winner. Second, with this information, some of you can leave (or ignore) this futile war and begin creating a new society. I'll explain how in the last chapter, titled *The Path Forward*.

Both sides think they are going to win, but they are mistaken. Why? Mainly because the Constitution is flawed and can't be fixed. The Constitution was written with the ideal of freedom as the foundation of America. Once that ideal lost its meaning, America was doomed. No longer is freedom the overriding ideal. Instead, we have devolved into a nation that is fighting over how to limit freedom. That fight is what this cold war is all about.

A few days ago, a *New York Times* editorial made the claim that free speech is no longer suitable for modern times. It came on the heels of the Department of Homeland Security (DHS) creating a new Disinformation Governance Board. The liberals believe that individual freedom is no longer important and must be curtailed. The Constitution has clearly failed us.

Ironically, it's not just the liberals who want to limit freedom. So do the conservatives. This is why neither side can win. The liberals want to limit freedom via increased government control. The conservatives want to limit freedom by keeping the status quo in place. They don't realize that the status quo limits the freedom of the disenfranchised (I will have much more to say on this subject).

A nation at war with itself is doomed, and that is our fate. America will be no more in its current state. The final outcome will be a transition into something new. Ironically, neither side has a clue of what is coming, and it has nothing to do with their political goals. Both sides want to limit freedom, and that surely is not our fate.

I should point out that it's not just America that is having internal problems at this time. In fact, the world is falling apart. Why? Because this is a transition point when the world changes. The initial change will be messy as our beliefs change. Currently, we are polarizing. Soon (5 years?) we will begin to come together as the truth is revealed. What truth? That separation is a lie.

I write about several subjects. Two of those are new age spirituality and politics. In this book, I will mix both subjects. This will antagonize many of you. So, I'm likely going to antagonize your politics and your spiritual beliefs. What is the saying: don't talk about politics or religion? Well, I'm going after both in this book.

I've written many new age spirituality books. I'm a 5th-level old soul. I'm highly lucid with regard to spiritual knowledge. Ironically, I'm also lucid with regard to politics. That's a very unusual combination. I've even written a new constitution that is available on Amazon called *Post America: A New Constitution*.

My highest level of expertise is spirituality, which I will be writing about in this book. I'm more of an amateur with regard to politics, but it has always been a passion of mine. In college, during the first week of my political science course, the professor asked if I was a Poly Sci major because I was talking a lot in class. I said no, and he asked why not? My reply was that I disagreed with both parties. To this day, I still do and subsequently don't vote. That's why I wrote a new constitution. Our system is broken, and I won't support a party that wants to limit freedom because that is a dead-end for humanity. I would prefer to see the political system replaced, which it will be.

Our current Constitution and political system are on the verge of failing. You may consider that statement hyperbole and fantasy, but the signs are everywhere if you are paying attention. I've been writing about the future since 1990. My goal is to help humanity move forward. My last book was titled *The Path*

Forward. Read that book next to have an idea of where we are heading as a civilization. I've also included my new constitution in Appendix One. This will provide additional ideas on how society will evolve.

My objective is to help humanity and to leave the world in a better place than I found it. Voting Democrat or Republican is not going to achieve that goal. In fact, it is going to do the opposite. If you read this book, you will understand why.

Don Durrett
May 2022

Chapter One

THE POLITICAL COLD WAR

This political cold war has its roots going back to the 1960s and the John F. Kennedy (JFK) administration. America was probably at its height if you consider all aspects of what America had accomplished. After World War II, America was the dominant economic and political power. We were the country that every other nation on the planet looked toward either as an example to emulate, or a country to admire.

Our industries were making everything the world needed. We were generating wealth and had no peer economically. Our standard of living was number one, and our political system and Constitution were the envy of the world.

Kennedy was clearly a moderate whose political allegiance was not to any agenda other than to make America the best it could be. The ideals of the Constitution still rang true, where freedom and opportunity were foundational anchors.

Yes, it's true that full freedom only applied to white men at that time, but Kennedy understood this problem needed to be resolved. He was clearly for civil rights and equality. If he had been given eight years in office, followed by another eight years by his brother Bobby, the ideal of freedom might have had a chance to survive. But his murder, along with the murder of his brother, ended any hope that the American ideal of freedom and equality would manifest for the entire population.

After Kennedy was killed, America slowly began to break down. Instead of focusing on America and its problems (many of which were being ignored), we went to war in Vietnam. A stupid war that cost many lives and led America astray. One thing it did was instill a military-oriented U.S. government that has remained to this day. Biden's 2023 budget recommends over $800 billion in military spending, with an increase to this year's military budget.

It hasn't mattered which party is in office — the military budget has been increasing since Kennedy was assassinated, and we have become the global policeman. One anomaly was Bill Clinton, who was trying to balance the budget in the 1990s. But after 9/11, big, ever-increasing military budgets have become the norm. Instead of focusing on America, we have continued to focus externally, almost exclusively for economic reasons.

While most Americans think the U.S. military is used to keep global peace and is defensive in nature, that has not been its true role since Vietnam. Instead, the military is used for economic reasons to ensure that America wields economic power throughout the world. While this might be a legitimate political strategy, it prevents a focus on our true problems. This has allowed our problems to become so large, so ingrained, that both parties no longer have a solution.

In my opinion, Kennedy was our last hope. He didn't want to go to war in Vietnam and start these endless wars. He wanted to focus on America's internal problems. Since then, the nation has steadily drifted apart from the moderate middle into extremes on the left and right. Ironically, neither extreme cares about freedom, not the full freedom that is necessary to create harmony in a nation. The liberals on the left, who are not the majority of the Democratic Party but have the loudest voice, seem to be intent on reducing freedom as fast as they can. Their agenda is quite apparent, which is to make the government as big and powerful as possible. It has become clear that their agenda is to remove freedom from individuals and give it to the government. They even label those who support Republicans as being anti-government.

Chapter One: The Political Cold War

The liberals want to have laws for everything that impinges on their agenda. They want high taxes for wealthy individuals (and corporations) to induce more equity, regardless if this hurts the economy. I read recently that Bernie Sanders, who I consider the father of the leftist-socialist movement, proposed a progressive tax on corporations up to 95%. This is insanity from an economic standpoint and stymies incentive to generate wealth. Instead of raising tax rates, we should create minimum tax levels based on gross income (all forms of income) for the super-rich. If an individual has a gross income above $1 million, then the minimum income tax would be 25% of the gross. With that in place, no one with a high income gets a free ride.

For corporations, we could also create a 15% minimum tax on operating cash flow, exempting those with less than 100 employees. If a large company is generating cash, then it should be paying taxes. If they are not generating cash, then we don't want to put them out of business, struggling to pay their taxes.

In addition to higher taxes, the liberals want to create a myriad of new laws to govern how we treat each other, how businesses can operate, how information is distributed, how vaccinations are required, how children are educated, how crime is punished, how guns are regulated, and many other categories. They want to become the arbiters of how we live our lives and run our businesses.

Each of these categories that liberals want to control could have its own chapter in this book. Incredibly, many of these were not even substantial issues a decade ago; for instance, how we educate our children. Today, school districts across the nation are teaching critical race theory (CRT). Amazingly, this theory presupposes that all white people are racists, and that racism is prevalent in America. The irony is that most white people are not racists.

CRT theory has inflamed ideas in the educational system about how America originated. The founding fathers, and the paternal white male-dominated society that followed, are now being ridiculed as being racists. Subsequently, what they built and created is being subjugated into irrelevance, with many liberals believing it needs to be replaced (our founding values). It is a very stealthy revolution to replace ideas of what the Constitution and Declaration of Independence mean.

Many liberals support defunding the police. When this started occurring, many in the country were startled. I was not. This is right out of their playbook of breaking down America and giving it a new identity. This is part of their war on America. They want a new America, and the police are viewed as tools of the status quo.

Ironically, once liberals obtain full control of government, they will embrace the police as their tool. They will take away everyone's guns and then militarize the police departments to maintain control. That is always the playbook of tyranny, which is what you get when governments become too powerful.

In addition to defunding the police, many liberals actually support crime. Why? Because it destabilized the status quo and gives them an opening to seize more power. In California, we have seen a series of laws that encourage crime. These laws have decreased penalties for petty theft and burglary. Is that by chance? No. They want anarchy, and we are seeing it.

Incredibly, the mainstream media (MSM) has supported their anarchy agenda. The Black Lives Matter (BLM) movement was given a free pass by the media. The damage to cities and businesses was immense, yet very few people were arrested or had trials. The MSM was much more interested in covering the January 6th riot at the Capitol building in Washington, D.C. Was that riot really more violent than many of the BLM protests? No, but yet, it was compared to 9/11 and even Pearl Harbor. Conversely, the BLM protests were treated with kid gloves by the media. In fact, much of the coverage was actually supportive of the protestors, regardless of the damage to property and businesses.

The MSM is clearly backing the liberals. Why? This is very clear: they identify with their political goals of equity that the conservative and Republican Party refuse to acknowledge is a problem. The MSM thinks the conservatives are the real threat to America. However, the fact remains that it is both groups who are the threat.

The problem with the government (using a liberal agenda) trying to determine what is best for society is that it is a slippery slope. Once laws are implemented, they rarely are removed. So, laws become laws on top of laws, and the government becomes all-powerful, and tyranny is quick to follow. Ironically, those who agree that government is good and necessary are quick to support the removal of freedom in the name of the higher good.

Many famous writers, such as George Orwell, have warned us that big government will lead to a dystopian future where freedom is highly controlled. Those who support large government call people who bring up this argument "conspiracy theorists." Well, count me one.

California, which is leading the nation toward leftist-socialist ideas, will soon be voting on a law that makes it illegal to release misinformation, including on social media. How insane is that? Someone could state an opinion and end up getting fined because a judge agrees that it is misinformation. This is America? No, but that is what it could turn into as government overreach increases.

The CEO of Twitter stated publicly that his objective is not to support free speech but instead healthy speech. Basically, he is stating that free speech does not apply to the Twitter platform and that they will determine what is healthy speech and what is allowed. That is the epitome of censorship, and we have witnessed quite a bit of it as a myriad of people have been kicked-off that platform for infringing on their rules.

One solution is to remove Twitter (or any social media platform) as the censor and instead use a third party, whereby the third party can uphold their rules without using a political bias. Moreover, all people who are kicked-off social media platforms should have the ability to appeal to an independent arbitration panel. All of this should be public and transparent, including speech that is censored.

Ironically, the large social media companies and government officials have backdoor communications regarding censoring information. That has to stop. This is more government overreach, with most of it being done in secret.

As you can tell from reading this far, I'm not a fan of the liberals. I like their goals but not their solutions. What America (or any nation) needs is more freedom and not less. Solutions have to support freedom because those are the only solutions that will create harmony.

Okay, what about their political cold war opponent, the conservatives? They think all we have to do is maintain the rule of law and a free market, and all will be well. Plus, a few more things, such as a strong military, balanced budget, limited government, immigration enforcement, the 2nd amendment, and low taxes. That's not everything, but a general overview. Where they fail badly is they ignore equity and equality. They don't see these as problems. Or, they see any attempt to increase equity as a path toward socialism/communism. A path they would rather fight against than support. This is why the progressive socialists came on the scene. They finally tired of the conservative intransigence.

It was inevitable that the progressive socialists would arise in America. The reason why is because freedom and equality are not compatible. This is clearly obvious and a lesson we have

Chapter One: The Political Cold War

recently learned. The more freedom you give to society, the more discrepant outcomes you will observe. Those with more resources and better schools will thrive. Those with higher IQs and better connections will thrive. Yet not everyone will thrive. Not only is free-market capitalism flawed, whereby monopolies tend to form, but freedom is also flawed.

Both of these must be addressed. The conservatives will agree to address monopolies to a certain extent, but even then, they will need to be dragged kicking and screaming. As for the flaw in freedom, most of them will disagree that such a flaw exists. In fact, they will claim any attempt to rectify that flaw is socialism, and some will label it communism.

Most conservatives are oblivious that this flaw is the downfall of their political philosophy. So, there is the basis of your political cold war. The liberals are trying to create a new society, whereby government knows what is best, and continuously implements laws where the government squeezes our freedom to where it no longer exists. And not only do liberals support the reduction of freedom, but the opposite of freedom, whereby government dictates how we live our lives. Ironically, liberals know this will likely create a dystopian society, but they don't care. They would rather destroy the values and foundation of America than continue with its current form. They believe that white people are in a position of privilege, which has to end, regardless of the outcome.

As you can see, to circle back to a point I made earlier in this chapter, the deeply ingrained problems of America are internal. By not dealing with them back in the 1960s and onward, we created a political quagmire.

How can the conservatives address the problem of equity and equality when liberals have defined it in irrational terms? By calling white Americans racists and privileged, it's a non-starter for conservatives. That's not a discussion the conservatives want to have. Conversely, the conservatives are focusing their attention on preventing the liberals from achieving their agenda. By fighting against the liberal agenda, there is no space or urgency to address the problem of equity and equality.

Ironically, what the liberals want (equity, equality, and opportunity) is pushing the conservatives to be recalcitrant. They are making it impossible for the conservatives to see any change that is possible in these areas. Conservatives want to keep the current economic system in place and fight against any new ideas of generating equity, equality, and opportunity. The problem for liberals is they have terrible solutions, but their understanding of the problem (lack of equity, equality, and opportunity) is good.

I have ideas for liberals, but they are just about out of time. First, demand free online education for K-12 and college. If a family can't get a good education for their child, or afford college, then an online option should be available. These free online college courses should be available to everyone. This will level the playing field. Note that there are already many free online college courses. They need to make these accredited toward a degree. What difference does it make which online course you took?

Second, they should demand more low-interest business loans for the lower and middle class that are guaranteed by government. Small business is a good way for the lower and middle class to climb up.

Third, they should demand a flatter pay scale, which will create instant raises for the lower and middle class. Depending on the size of the firm, the scale should be around 10 to 1 from top to bottom. The key here is the bottom pay levels will be much higher than they are today, and the top levels will be much lower.

I have ideas for conservatives as well. They need to acknowledge that they are limiting the freedom of the middle and lower class by restricting opportunity. This is perpetrated by maintaining the status quo. The liberals are right when they say that equity does not exist on a societal level. That limitation of equity is the equivalent of limiting freedom. Those without equity are generally living paycheck to paycheck, watching the American Dream slip away.

Opportunities are not plentiful for the lower class. Throughout America, your zip code often determines your future. That is limited freedom, and that limitation is what the conservatives are often fighting to maintain. Ironically, conservatives do not realize that they are fighting the wrong battle. If they want to maintain their freedom, then they have to extend it to more Americans. If they limit others' freedom, then they will end up finding their freedom limited.

Ironically, the liberals are fighting for equity while at the same time fighting to curtail freedom via a more expansive government. What is the point of achieving equity if you don't have the freedom to enjoy it?

The conservatives are fighting to limit or stop the expansion of government, while at the same time attempting to achieve their objectives (stated earlier). Ironically, one of those objectives is to prevent any changes in how equity is obtained. It is this final agenda where the conservatives are failing badly and don't even realize it.

I hope I am being lucid enough for you to realize the predicament that America finds itself in today. The liberals are trying to achieve a better America when, in actuality, they are ruining it (by removing freedom). The conservatives are trying to maintain an American ideal that they think is working, when in fact, it is utterly failing. In fact, they are the reason the progressive socialists exist.

If we had had eight years of the Kennedys, the leftist-socialists likely would have never come into existence. Moreover, the conservatives would never have veered so far to the right as to ignore the necessity of social equity and social opportunity. It is ironic to me that the conservatives do not see that if you do not have social equity and social opportunity, that you are allowing a cancer to grow to such an extent as to destroy the life around you. Hasn't that yet become obvious?

Ironically, while the lower class begins to lash out at society with a plethora of crime and violence, the conservatives point their finger at them and say they are the problem. The conservatives are blind to the fact that their intransigence against social equity and social opportunity is the very cause of this outcome.

The argument I always hear is that you can't create a utopia, so why try? The second argument I hear is that you are always going to have social classes of rich and poor people. But these are straw man arguments that don't hold water. Moreover, if you don't wake up to this fact, you are going to wake up to an America that is a third-world country strewn with violence, corruption, and crime. You better start dealing with this problem, and soon, because the clock is ticking, and you are quickly running out of time.

Unfortunately, the problem of inequity and lack of opportunity can only be solved in the middle, whereby the liberals give up their insanity that the government has all the answers, and the conservatives give up their insanity that inequity is part of life, and opportunity either already exists or can't be fixed.

Do you see? Both sides in this political cold war have lost their way. As Einstein said so eloquently, you can't solve a problem by doing the same thing over and over. You have to try something different. Unfortunately, that's not how our political parties think today. In fact, both want to continue doing the same thing over and over, which is insanity personified.

*****

Chapter One: The Political Cold War

Let's look at where this insanity is leading us, and why both agendas are doomed. The conservatives want to prevent the lower and middle class from getting a hand up from government programs that can achieve social equity and social equality. They are content for both of these classes to struggle. The middle class has been shrinking for 50 years, and yet the conservatives don't care, or at least don't care enough to try something different.

The liberals are so angry at the conservative intransigence that they don't care if they have to rip up the Constitution to create change. As far as they are concerned, the Constitution was written by a bunch of racists who don't care about equity and equality. This is why we are continually witnessing attempts to dismantle the Constitution via new laws. The vax mandates are a good example. Clearly, it is not constitutional to force an experimental vaccine onto the public. But that, in fact, is what happened. The liberals were 100% in favor of this approach, because they deemed it for the greater good, regardless of constitutional issues. The Constitution carried zero weight in their mind.

The vax mandates were not constitutional, so they were implemented via a workaround for worker safety. They can't force a citizen to take a vaccine, but they can force an employee by calling it a safety measure. All of the elected officials in Washington D.C. are employees of the government, yet they were exempt from these mandates. Irony? Yep. Big-time irony. Even employees at the Center for Disease Control (CDC) were exempt.

Exemptions abounded, but vax mandates went forward anyway. Biden tried to force large employers to have their employees vaccinated, but the Supreme Court said that was unconstitutional. Ironically, even after that ruling, the Administration considered it a political ruling and hailed it as incorrect, and they disagreed with it. Many liberals wanted to mandate the vaccine for everyone.

Such is their mentality that the greater good is the number one driver of social policy and not freedom.

The vax mandates and the passion of the liberals to implement them correlated with another political issue they hold dearly, which is government control of information on social media and the MSM. This is another slippery slope into a dystopian world. Who can define what is misinformation with regard to an experimental vaccine when information is fluid? Nobody, and thus we have had a dearth of quality information regarding COVID-19.

As far as the liberals were concerned, the government was the arbiter of vaccine information, and anything contrary to this authentic source was misinformation. However, when has the government ever been a reliable source of information? The media's main job is to do reporting that confirms what the government is saying, and to question everything. Yet, the media were effectively banned from doing their job, except for reporting verbatim what the Biden Administration and government departments and agencies were releasing.

Doctors and researchers were releasing their own information regarding COVID-19 data and were getting labeled as releasing misinformation. Many doctors and researchers were losing their jobs for releasing information. It was as if there was complete censorship by the government. The liberals were 100% behind this war on misinformation. They were 100% behind the government. There were no calls for investigative reporting to double-check what the government was saying. It was all accepted verbatim.

This became a war on the first amendment between the liberals and the conservatives. In fact, the war rages today. The liberals what to tear up the Constitution and pretend the first amendment does not exist. They want to decide what can be said and what can't. Again, this is a very slippery slope where the government decides what is good for society. More importantly, the government gets to control what information is released by determining what is misinformation.

It seems like the media has now agreed to follow the government narratives, and anything that veers away from these narratives is labeled misinformation. That is a scary precedent and renders the media meaningless and unreliable. The media was never meant to be the voice of government. We learned that fact during the cold war when *Pravda* was the propaganda voice of the Soviet Union. We used to make fun of *Pravda*, and now we are doing the same thing. Again, another slippery slope we have created.

I recently read where the *New York Times* was calling free speech nonsensical. They want to destroy free speech in the same manner that they want to destroy the 2nd amendment. I'm not a gun lover and don't own one, but I do respect the Constitution. I do think that it is not yet time to get rid of everyone's guns, but I do think a time will come when it makes sense. Perhaps in a generation or two, when peace breaks out and government tyranny is no longer a threat. But the combination of destroying both the first and 2nd amendment is right at the heart of this political cold war. Those are two issues that both sides will not budge over.

We have reached an era where debates over conspiracy theories are threatened, and opinions are no longer allowed if they are viewed as misinformation. That's a scary development. The control of information seems to be viewed as necessary by liberals. They want to tell us how to live and not to ask questions. Dystopian? Sure. And it is also something that is generating this political cold war.

So, both sides are bringing out the worst in each other. America is at war with itself. It's not pretty, and it will not end in victory for either side. Instead, it will end in failure for both. Neither wants to admit it, but both sides are bringing us down. The American era is over. Now we have to figure out what replaces it. You can support the left or the right, or you can find a solution. But you can't do both.

* * * *

I want to reiterate that when I use the term liberal or conservative, I am not referring to moderates. There are many moderates who disagree with the extreme views of the far-left or far-right. This book is intended to suggest that extreme elements of both parties have taken over the narratives/platforms of both parties. The moderates have been marginalized, and what they want is no longer a leading voice on most matters.

A good example is the 2nd Amendment. Most moderate liberals are okay with the 2nd Amendment and only want to see laws that make it more difficult for criminals to obtain guns. The far-left is much more intent on making all assault weapons illegal to own. If this type of law is passed and approved by a liberal Supreme Court (if we ever get one), it effectively shreds the 2nd Amendment to be meaningless.

Chapter Two

THE TWO PARTIES

Let's look at history to see how this political cold war came about. After JFK was assassinated in 1963, this war was put in motion. In 1964, Barry Goldwater was the Republican presidential nominee. I consider him the father of the modern conservative movement. He put in motion what exists today as the Republican Party. His platform is the epitome of what infuriates the liberals today. He had very little affinity with the lower class or minorities. He wanted white American men to continue to dominate society and flourish. He wanted more of the same.

What the Republican Party did not want in 1964, was change. That mindset is still with us today. All of the leftist-progressive ideas are rejected without a second thought. This intransigence can be connected back to 1964. That was when the conservatives categorically rejected the idea that America was broken and needed to change with regard to equity and equality. The evidence is in their refusal to support the Civil Rights Act. It was proposed in June 1963 by President Kennedy and was initially rejected by a filibuster in the Senate. It was later resurrected and passed by President Johnson in 1964, although 130 conservative House members and 27 conservative Senators voted no.

From Goldwater's viewpoint, America was not broken and did not need to change. What was broken was the idea that change was needed. This conservative intransigence would continue to fight against a multitude of issues that minorities, women, LGBTQ, and the poor continue to fight for today.

It's interesting that 1964 was close to the height of American exceptionalism. At that time, America had no peers economically. We had the highest standard of living in the world. The rest of the world was still catching up. Even our education system had not yet begun to rot.

From this perspective, it is easy to see why Goldwater thought leftist-progressive ideas were a pox on America. We were literally the leader of the world in everything. That was an era when the rest of the world imported our products, and not vice-versa.

It is easy to see why conservatives were blind to the vitriol they were getting ready to unleash. By assuming that America wasn't broken, they allowed a festering problem to turn into a raging political war. It started in the 1960s with Goldwater, but it was galvanized during the 1980s under Reagan.

I lived through that period, turning twenty in 1980. I remember the Reagan platform and his trickle-down economics. His focus was on a strong economic America, which was accomplished through lower taxes, free trade, and budget deficits that added stimulus. He gave birth to globalism, to the detriment of the middle class. Ross Perot correctly called it that whooshing sound of jobs leaving the country. The conservatives were pro-business and not pro-worker. What made America great to them was the success of businesses.

The economy was a thing of beauty from 1982 until 1998, growing at a rapid pace. But during that period, all of the leftist-progressive ideas were shunned into the background and festered. The pro-business economic system was such a juggernaut that nothing else could get oxygen in Washington. Bill Clinton, a Democrat, was elected from 1992 to 2000, but he was basically a moderate Republican and passed zero legislation for the disenfranchised that had any impact.

So, from Goldwater's platform in 1964 (as the Republican presidential nominee), we ended up getting 20 years of conservative values (from 1980 to 2000). Those 20 years ruined America (I will explain why). Ironically, they were America's strongest years economically. Many, many Americans became affluent during that period. But even more were left behind, including the lower and middle class.

Why it ruined America was because we should have begun fixing the income (equity) and opportunity (equality) gap in the 1960s. By ignoring these problems and then allowing conservative values to become ingrained from 1980 to 2000, we achieved political gridlock, which gave birth to the leftist-progressive movement inspired by Bernie Sanders in 2016.

By ignoring the equity and equality problems for so long, we allowed a barrier to be raised between the parties. The moderate portions of each party were hollowed out. Those who were left to deal with these issues after 2016 were in no position to make any progress. In fact, those leading the charge to fix these issues (the leftist- progressives) only had radical ideas based on collectivism. They wanted to solve the problem from the left, which was untenable (more on this later).

My point is that because the conservatives were able to set the agenda for the country from 1980 to 2000, once we arrived in this century, we were politically trapped and destined to fail. After 9/11 in 2001 and the Great Financial Crisis in 2008, the conservatives were beginning to realize that the country was in trouble economically. They were in no mood to focus on the equity and equality issues of the lower and middle class. Their desire was to get the economy back on its feet and to maintain the agenda that made America great from 1980 to 2000 (a pro-business mindset).

The Democrats were basically left without a counterpart to discuss equity (income) and equality (opportunity) issues. When

Obama came into office in 2008, his platform was supposed to give the country hope, especially for those who had been left behind. But during his eight years in office, he continued the conservative economic system of globalism. He did nothing to change the disparity of income and opportunity. Why not? Because Washington had become gridlocked with partisan rancor. The liberals did not have any moderate Republicans to align with to fix income and opportunity issues.

The momentum of the conservative agenda from 1980 to 2000 was so strong that not even the MSM discussed the problems of the middle and lower class until Bernie Sanders brought them up in 2016. It was almost as if the Democratic Party was hypnotized by the Republican agenda from 1980 until 2016. They were frozen to act, but the vitriol and animosity against the conservative agenda was spreading throughout the Democratic Party and MSM.

Once Bernie appeared as a presidential candidate with his leftist-progressive platform, it was too late. He exposed the problems of inequity and lack of opportunity, but he didn't have answers. Not only did Bernie not have the answers, but neither did anyone else. As a nation, the answers were elusive or untenable. I will have more to say about Bernie in a separate chapter. What I want to emphasize here is that the conservatives made a tremendous blunder in the 1960s. By assuming that America was great, they missed that America was still a work in progress. They understood that freedom and capitalism are important, but what they missed is that without opportunity for all, not everyone is free. And if you limit part of the population's freedom and opportunity, eventually that part of society will bring down the rest. Such is the state of America today.

In short, Goldwater and the conservatives brought down America. It's ironic that as I write this, conservatives are trying to save America using the same agenda that created this mess.

Chapter Two: The Two Parties

In fact, Donald Trump is currently (in early 2022) giving rallies called Save America. They are right to be concerned. America's future indeed is at risk. Sadly, it cannot be saved. At least not in its current form. Perhaps it was always destined to fail.

Another theme that conservative candidates utilize is to defend freedom. Isn't it interesting that this theme implies a war of some type? So, on a certain level, they are acknowledging that a war with the left exists. Ironically, what they really mean is that they will defend the status quo. They have no intention of defending the freedom (to achieve the American Dream) that largely does not exists for the lower class.

Chants of USA, USA, USA at the Republican presidential nomination convention are chants of satisfaction with the status quo. These are not chants of American exceptionalism, which has waned since the 1960s. We are no longer the pre-eminent nation that we once were that deserved accolades.

Ironically, the Democratic Party has begun making these chants now that this political cold war has begun. They recognize what these chant really symbolize, which is our party is the best. It's no longer a chant for America. It's a chant for the party itself.

There are no conservatives speaking about the real culprit of America's decay, which is the lack of economic opportunity and equality (which will create equity) for the lower and middle class. We are still stuck in the same conservative pablum that everyone can be successful through hard work. This is such baloney, when it is so obvious that the zip code where you are born is the number one indicator of the success you will achieve.

I know that my zip code played a huge role in my success. In fact, if I failed, it surely would have been my fault because I had ample opportunity. That is clear for me to see in hindsight. How many school-age kids in America today have a similar opportunity that I had? Maybe 20%. Perhaps a bit more. Clearly, opportunity is shrinking. Why is that? Is the same old Goldwater–Reagan conservative platform going to reverse that? Not a chance. And that is why the liberals are so angry, and also why the MSM has joined the liberal cause. It's obvious to them as well, that something needs to change, and the old status quo has to go.

The reason the Democrats have moved left is that there are no more Republicans in the middle to discuss issues with. That part of the Republican Party has been hollowed out. Their only recourse was to move left and go it alone. Unfortunately, by moving left, they made Republicans even more recalcitrant to talk with them. And voila, the political cold war was born.

Most conservatives will disagree with what I have written in this book. They are emphatic that they are right. They will think Reagan was a great president and his policies were good for this country. Many of them have similar affections for Trump. Not until history is finally written a few decades from now will the blunder of the conservatives become so apparent.

In hindsight, it's easy to see why they got it wrong. They didn't have an example. How could they know that the human soul demands to be free? And that their political agenda essentially prevented this outcome for many? They believed it was the best political system. And if you look at the economic benefits from 1945 to 1965, and 1980 to 2000, it is hard to argue. It is only when you can see the whole picture that it becomes apparent.

The Republican Party brought in women and minorities in an attempt to make it appear that it was a party for everyone. However, these groups were only allowed into the club if they embraced the Goldwater–Reagan conservative ideals. My parents and most of my family voted Republican. I was aghast growing up that this is what I was supposed to support. I rebelled. But when I looked

Chapter Two: The Two Parties

at my other option, the Democrats, I quickly realized that I was screwed. I had no one to support.

The Republican Party (conservatives) supports, in no particular order, patriotism, individualism, meritocracy, family, law and order, military, business, low taxes, limited government, reducing business regulations, freedom, the 2nd amendment, hard work, education, morality, abortion laws, Christianity, immigration laws, free speech, the Constitution, and conservative ideals.

Notice some of the important issues not on that list, such as equality, equity, civil rights, and LGBTQ rights. If the conservatives had their way, the Civil Rights Act would not have passed in 1964, and blacks would have had to wait longer for the right to eat at all restaurants and sleep at all hotels in America. It's not hyperbole to think it could have been delayed for another decade or so if the conservatives had their way.

From 1964 until 1980, the Republican Party remained moderate, with the conservative wing biding its time. After Goldwater in 1964, we didn't get another conservative candidate until Ronald Reagan in 1980. Some would argue that Nixon was a conservative, but if you look at the government programs he created, he was more moderate than both of the Bush presidencies. For instance, he created the Environmental Protection Agency and other government programs that today are lauded by liberals.

Everything that had been marinating regarding conservatism since 1964 exploded onto the scene in the 1980s. Most Republicans think this was a good thing. They loved Reagan. Unbeknownst to them, this was in actuality the undoing of America. The seeds of dissension that are with us today.

Reagan cemented what Goldwater put in motion. The two of them laid the foundation for what has been the Republican Party for the past 42 years. The moderates have been pushed out, and the conservatives have reigned. They even gave a name to those Republicans who were not conservative enough: RINOs (Republicans in name only).

Newt Gingrich was the number three player in the creation of the conservative movement, although you could also include Rush Limbaugh and his huge radio audience. Newt released *The Contract with America* in the early 1990s. That was the height of the conservative movement. In fact, shortly after that period, the Republican Party began to wane. Bill Clinton won both presidential elections in the 1990s, and then Barrack Obama won two more, removing the momentum that Reagan created.

The Republican Party thought they were America's party after the 1980s, but it was not to be. Why? It was because of their Achilles heel of ignoring the lower class, social justice, social equity, and opportunity for all. By ignoring these issues, they were actually fighting against them.

The Democratic Party remained moderate all the way until 2016 and was mostly a non-factor in pursuing these important issues. In hindsight, it is amazing they remained moderate for such an extended period. There are a lot of similarities between the delay of the emergence of the conservative movement after Goldwater's candidacy, and the delay of the leftist-progressive wing of the Democratic Party emerging. Like Goldwater's conservatives, the Democrat's liberals marinated for a long period before finally forming a movement.

The leftist-progressives remained dormant during the 1980s, when Reagan was a juggernaut, and their voice was smothered out. Then under Bill Clinton, they had to let him lead as a moderate. Like Reagan, Clinton's voice smothered them out. Leftist-progressive ideas of today were barely whispered during those two decades. You had a few voices, such as Noam Chomsky, but they were drowned out and marginalized.

Chapter Two: The Two Parties

By the time we got to this century, the liberals did not have a voice or a leader. There were no far-left politicians that had a national voice. The poor and disenfranchised were left rudderless. There was the black caucus, but it was largely a fringe group with no political influence. Ironically, Bill Clinton, in the 1990s, actually signed into law a harsh crime bill and a welfare reform bill that penalized the poor. Both of these laws were slaps in the face of what the liberals support today.

In the 1980s and 1990s, very few women were elected to national government, especially in the Senate, which remained mostly a white men's club. Finally, this century, more women and minorities were elected. Ironically, Barrack Obama, a black man, governed as a moderate from 2008 until 2016. He never allowed the party to move to the left and address leftist-progressive issues that are embraced so strongly today by liberals. Once again, the liberals could not find a voice. We got Obamacare, but that came from the support of the entire party and not just the left wing. Obama was no more leftist-socialist than Bill Clinton.

That all changed in 2016, when the political cold war emerged. Enter Bernie Sanders, the father of the leftist-progressive movement. When he ran against Hillary to get the Democratic nomination, the party hated him, as did the media. They wanted the Democratic Party to remain moderate, which they thought was necessary to defeat Donald Trump. Bernie was treated badly by the party, which clearly supported Hillary Clinton.

I believe that Bernie would have beat Trump, but that is conjecture. He brought a renewed energy to the party and exposed all that had been marinating for decades. The Democratic Party had not been fighting for the right issues, the heart of it being social equity and equality, along with economic opportunity. He ignited a movement. Thousands came to his rallies, with most of them being young. Many of Bernie's supporters stayed home on election day.

I wonder what the Democratic turnout would have been in 2016 if he had won the nomination. Hillary won the Democratic nomination, but she was such a flawed candidate, and her rallies were tepid at best. There was very little enthusiasm for her campaign, and her platform was basically a clone of the Obama administration. Obama had very few accomplishments, so what was Hillary going to do differently?

Even in losing the Democratic nomination in 2016, Bernie ignited a movement with staying power. He also ignited a war with the conservatives. More than that, he ignited a war to change the country and give it a new identity, thereby shredding the Constitution. After Hillary lost to Trump, the Democratic Party rallied around Bernie's platform of leftist-progressive ideas.

The Democratic Party became energized with a sense of urgency in 2016. First, it had a mission to fight against Trump, the first conservative president since Reagan. This fight became an all-out war. Trump was the Devil incarnate and had to go. Second, they adopted Bernie's agenda of defeating conservatives by controlling government. This meant all bipartisanship ended. The end goal was to control government and marginalize the conservatives.

Bernie is a full-on socialist, but the liberals and the MSM didn't care. They recognized that his strategy to reshape America and marginalize the conservatives was the best approach. It became a stealth campaign to transform American political power. It was a brazen attempt to end the Goldwater–Reagan agenda. If it meant destroying journalism and even destroying America itself, so be it. They were going to do to the Republicans what Goldwater and Reagan had done to them, which was to suck the oxygen out of their platform and make it irrelevant. To do that, they had to take control of the government. So, it became an all-out war. This is where we are today.

Now you know why the liberals possibly stole the 2020 election. When you are fighting a war, anything goes. The documentary *2000 Mules* shows how it could have been stolen (unless it is fake). The documentary shows how investigators used cell phone tracking data to identify 2000 cellphones (in five key swing states) that repeatedly interacted with nonprofit organizations and mail-in ballot drop-off sites. Plus, they confirmed their data using video. Anyone who watches that documentary comes away with an OMG (oh my God!) moment.

We have had three huge government conspiracies in my lifetime. All three are conspiracies because they were covered up. The first was the JFK assassination. The second was 9/11. Now the third and final straw was the 2020 election. America's bad karma has finally reached a breaking point. Three strikes, and you're out.

Amazingly, at least 30% of Americans (one poll showed 40%) believe the 2020 election was stolen. Instead of forming a committee to investigate election irregularities, liberals called it the big lie, and disregarded all reported irregularities.

Instead of investigating the election, they formed a committee to investigate the January 6th riot, calling it a planned insurrection. The narratives were blatant and one-sided. Instead of giving any credence to election fraud, anyone who brought it up was pushing the big lie.

Incredibly, the January 6th committee to investigate the so-called insurrection ignored all election irregularities. Instead, they reinforced the idea that the election had zero irregularities. The dozens of stories about these irregularities were ignored. It reminded me of the Warren Commission and the 9-11 Commission. All three failed to uncover the truth.

So, you can imagine the conservative's anger over the lack of a thorough Congressional investigation regarding the 2020 elections. Conversely, the liberals are just as angry regarding the looming decision to overturn Roe v. Wade, which will make abortion illegal in many states.

These two issues have made the relationship between conservatives and liberals incendiary. But that is just the tip of the iceberg, as both parties view America from a different philosophical lens.

* * * *

Bernie's plan of expanding government as the solution to our problems was embraced by the liberals and MSM. This was the underlying foundation of the attacks on Trump during his four years in office. Trump was not going to expand government, so he was the enemy of the liberals and MSM. He was hurting America by restricting government (the Goldwater–Reagan agenda) and not allowing it to address the leftist-progressive issues of equity, equality, and opportunity. The liberals and MSM had enough of the Goldwater–Reagan agenda. They were done. Their patience had reached its limit.

This was clear for all to see as *CNN* and *MSNBC* both changed their programming to specifically attack Trump nearly 24/7. Over 90% of the coverage of Trump on those two stations was negative, with most of it outright verbal attacks.

Trump became the symbol of all that was wrong with the Goldwater–Reagan agenda. All of the marinating of leftist-progressive ideas came tumbling down on his head. He was the most reviled president of all time. To this day, most liberals only have negative views of him. Ironically, he wasn't that bad of a president, avoiding war for four years and managing to avoid an economic crisis. But in the liberal's eyes, he was the scourge of the Earth. Why? They had begun their political cold war, and they intended to win. And what did winning look like? A large, expanding government that addressed the leftist-progressive gamut of programs and taxes needed to transform America into a new identity.

In the same vein that the conservatives misunderstood the importance of equality and equity for all, the liberals misunderstood the importance of individual freedom and individual sovereignty. For this reason, Bernie was leading his flock down a dangerous path, a path with only a dystopian outcome. His followers, and subsequently, the liberals and MSM, thought his message of expanded government was what the country needed. What they misconstrued was that his platform was a false pretense. He did not have the answers to our problems. He only had good descriptions of the problems. And that is the crux of the leftist-progressives today. They only understand the problems, which Bernie so eloquently pointed out.

Basically, Bernie waved his arms and hands (one of his successful tactics) and described why the conservative movement was limiting many of their freedom and robbing them of equity and equality. He was spot on, but that was only half the story. The other half was the solution, which he didn't have. His solution was to destroy America in its current form and create a big powerful government that the Democratic Party controls. Again, it was a false pretense. He was a fake. He was not going to give people freedom, equity, and equality. Quite the opposite, which is what all large tyrannical governments end up doing. How many examples do we need before we figure this out?

Not surprisingly, Bernie's exposure of the conservative movement ignited the leftist-socialist wing of the party (also called progressives and the woke mob) to be born. This wing has bought into his false pretense that the answer to our problems is expanded government run by the Democratic Party. They have taken up the mantle and plan to implement his vision. Amazingly, the MSM is helping them to achieve this goal.

You could make an argument that the conservative movement began this war in the 1980s and has been fighting it ever since. The liberals did not realize this war was taking place until Bernie pointed it out. Historically, this political war that began in 1980 is not recognized as such, but it was and is indeed real if you are paying attention. The conservative's war was to implement the Goldwater–Reagan agenda and suck the political life out of the liberals. They have been quite successful at carrying out that agenda, which has been in place since 1980.

Today, we have a new, more aggressive conservative movement that has arisen to contest this new leftist-progressive movement. Their objective is simple: keep the Goldwater–Reagan agenda in place. The clash between both movements has created a stunningly virulent political civil war. Both sides are willing to die over their beliefs, so this will probably get violent before it ends. Antifa has emerged, so the violence is already here. The MSM and Federal Bureau of Investigation are highly worried about white supremacist groups becoming violent. It will probably happen if the liberals are too successful with their agenda.

Neither side cares about compromising. This is a political fight that will continue until America unravels. The political division that exists today will not be closed. In fact, it will only widen. America is now on a single path, which is the end of America as we know it. There are no more forks in the road where America can solve its problems. We had a chance to take a different path in the 1960s, and we took the wrong turn.

What you are reading, no one wants to talk about. For instance, have you read anywhere that America is at war with itself? It's

Chapter Two: The Two Parties

obviously happening, yet the MSM does not want to write about it. Now, why is that? It's because both sides in this war have narratives that they want to push, and being at war is not part of those narratives. The narrative of both sides is that they will win and fix America. This is not possible, and I'll explain why in subsequent chapters.

In the next chapter, let's look at some of those narratives.

Chapter Three

THEIR NARRATIVES

To understand the narratives of conservatives and liberals, all we have to do is watch *Fox News* for the conservative narratives and *CNN* for the liberal narratives. These two cable channels are clearly supporters of these two factions. To say that they are both biased is an understatement. They are cheerleaders for their side. Their niche is to attract those who support a specific political faction. They are no longer news shows. Instead, they have become political shows. They can put "news" in their name, but that title has become irrelevant.

Fox News was the first cable news channel to embrace supporting a political faction. They tapped into the large group of people who supported the conservative wing of the Republican Party. Talk radio was the progenitor, beginning with Rush Limbaugh in the late 1980s, and then a plethora of conservative talk radio shows ever since. That huge audience had to eventually emerge on TV, and it did with *Fox News*.

The narrative from day one at *Fox News* is that Reagan and Newt Gingrich are heroes that we can't forget. In fact, Newt Gingrich was a regular guest for many years. The regular programming is either verbal attacks targeted at their enemy, the liberal left, or drumbeats for the Republic platform. They are fighting against any changes to the Goldwater–Reagan agenda and have been for many years. Their narrative is directly linked to the Reagan Era and the conservative Limbaugh philosophy, which is still evident on a daily basis if you are paying attention.

Those narratives are firmly based on conservative principles that have not changed much since 1980. Let's list a few, although it won't be close to a comprehensive list: 1) Businesses are most efficient and successful from low taxes and low regulations. 2) Society works best when individuals succeed through hard work and determination. 3) The Constitution and the rule of law are the basis for the greatness of America. 4) Opportunity exists for everyone who works hard enough. 5) Abortion is wrong. 6) The military comprises patriots who are heroes. 7) Our military must always be well-funded to remain the best in the world. 8) Illegal immigration is wrong. 9) The family is the backbone of America. 10) The 2nd Amendment is not negotiable. 11) Free speech is guaranteed by the Constitution. 12) High moral character is a virtue that we should all aspire toward. 13) America is the greatest country on Earth. 14) Socialism and communism are a scourge. 15) Government size and power should be limited.

You will never hear anyone who works for *Fox News* contradict any of those 15 narratives. And depending on which party is in office, *Fox News* anchors will either spend the majority of their time attacking the Democratic president or supporting the Republican president and the Republican platform. Currently, Biden is president, so the spiel is mostly attacks aimed at him or his policies.

The verbal attacks from *Fox News* anchors mostly have merit, and they feel good about their work. However, what they are missing with their coverage is that they are also doing harm to society. The conservative narratives they are pushing are creating as much of a problem as the liberal agenda they are attacking. Both are bringing the nation down.

Okay, it's time for me to bring in spirituality to defend my statements. How are conservatives creating problems? The answer is that there is only one consciousness of which we all share. This is the consciousness of the Creator or God; take your choice for the term you prefer. There is only one consciousness. We perceive ourselves to have our own consciousness and to be separate from others and separate from God. This is an illusion. There is no separation from anything because everything is consciousness, and everything is connected. Even the air you breathe.

* * * *

I understand that these spiritual concepts have no place in politics. But to understand the state of America and the state of politics, these concepts are necessary. Without them, you won't be able to see the whole picture. I ask that you read the rest of the book as if it is a theory, and then see where it leads. I promise it will be interesting.

* * * *

The acceptance of separation (between people and between anything) is the denial of God. Why? Because separation does not exist. Separation is a lie. Conversely, it is the recognition of God in ourselves that allows us to recognize the God in others, and the conscious connection to others. The recognition that we are all one consciousness obliterates the conservative ideology. It makes it meaningless and exposes the attacks on the liberal left as the wrong approach. Sure, the liberals are void of solutions, but the answer is not to attack their solutions, but instead to voice the correct solutions.

Once you realize that we are all one and that separation does not exist, you realize that true freedom is the only political ideology that makes sense. So, all political aspirations have to be focused on generating freedom and harmony for all.

Don, what are you talking about? You said earlier that freedom and Democracy are not compatible. That is only true if you are stuck in separation. Once you realize that everyone is one with the Creator and is an eternal soul, everything changes. If everyone is one with the Creator, then everyone is basically a clone of God. Everyone is one big family. Racism becomes mute. How can you be racist to a family member who is an eternal soul? Violence becomes mute. Why would you hurt another eternal soul, another family member?

Once the lie of separation is exposed, politics division become mute. At that time (in the near future), gratitude, compassion, love, humility, patience, and generosity begin to manifest throughout society. A total transformation of humanity unfolds.

Do you now see why both sides in this political cold war are doomed to fail? Let me fill you in with a few more spiritual truths. I'm a 5th-level old soul. I've lived over 1,000 lifetimes, and I'm highly lucid with spiritual knowledge. This is actually an advanced planet spiritually. It's not easy to come here. The average person on this planet has lived over 100 lifetimes. There are not many new souls here, with very few incarnations of experience.

Most souls on this planet are fairly evolved and are here to experience what humanity is about to find out. We are here to experience something that is quite rare in the cosmos. This planet and its civilization are about to ascend to a higher level of spiritual awareness.

In 2019, we passed the knowledge barrier. This changes everything. Now we will begin to advance at a rapid pace, with new technologies appearing. Science, for the first time, will be able to study consciousness. They will eventually prove what I just told you, that there is only one consciousness that we all share. Unfortunately, it will take science a few more decades to prove this fact. However, as they make strides toward this discovery, most of humanity will have already accepted it as fact.

I awoke in 1989, that was two years after the Harmonic Convergence in 1987, which put the whole plan in motion. We decided as a civilization to move forward. We made this decision as a collective consciousness. By 2012, we had succeeded. We had raised our consciousness high enough to proceed. Then it was only a matter of time until we crossed the knowledge barrier. It is no coincidence that COVID-19 appeared one year after we crossed, and the world has been chaotic ever since.

The chaos will continue for a few more years as society breaks away from old patterns of thinking. Spirituality is rising now at a rapid pace. By the end of this decade, what I have written in the book will become real. Many will perceive separation to be a lie, and oneness to be the truth. This won't happen to everyone all at once. In fact, it will be a slow process, with each individual awaking at their one schedule.

The awakening has already begun, with about 2% to 3% already fully awake, and *know* that separation is a lie. Ironically, it will be the hardcore religious fundamentalists who are the last to awaken. They will hold on tightly to their beliefs. This isn't that surprising when you know that young souls are more apt to be attracted to religion. Old souls, such as myself, tend to be inner-directed, and are less apt to follow doctrine. Krishnamurti said it best: to paraphrase, if you accept a doctrine, then you place yourself in a box, trapped by the doctrine's beliefs.

As eternal souls, we are free. Our core is love, but also freedom. Unconditional love is freedom. Ideas remove freedom. You have to be very careful with ideas. Otherwise, you will remove freedom and not even realize it. Words, beliefs, and ideas are all ways that we control each other's freedom. We can do it to each other, and government can do it to all of us.

The only idea you need to hold is I AM. Once you venture away from that idea, you begin a slippery slope. The purpose of incarnations is to learn that simple lesson. That is the lesson you are currently learning and likely have no clue to that fact. This planet is a school for souls. A school that teaches us one thing. That love is all that exists, and that there is only one consciousness. I AM.

Now, why am I writing this book? Why mix politics and spirituality? To awaken a few souls. If you are ready to awaken and you read this book, then you will. And if you are ready to awaken in this lifetime, then this book could help for that outcome.

Let me summarize a few spiritual ideas before we return to politics. First, every soul on this planet is one with the Creator. In fact, there is no separation between anything and the Creator. This is impossible because there is only one consciousness that is shared by everything. All is connected, and all is one.

Each soul is an aspect of the Creator that is evolving to learn one lesson, which is that only love exists, which is our core. This lesson requires many lifetimes, which are spent incarnating on various physical planets. Our true existence, what you could call "home," is on the non-physical spiritual planes, where we exist as pure energy. These planes can be called heaven because joy is pervasive and constant. Those who have near-death experiences rarely want to return to their bodies. Why? Because of the deep love they felt when not in their bodies.

Spirituality really comes down to a few simple ideas: 1) We are one with God. 2) We are eternal beings. 3) There is no separation between anything. 4) There is only one consciousness. 5) We

Chapter Three: Their Narratives

are incarnating in these bodies to learn one lesson, which is that only love is real. 6) It requires many, many lifetimes to learn this lesson. 7) We do it because we want to; it's our choice. 8) Everyone incarnates with a plan, called a soul contract. 9) Everyone is learning something, which becomes soul growth. 10) No lifetime is wasted because all is perfection.

Those ten statements are the truth. They are not my opinion. My credentials for validating that information is that not only am I a 5th-level old soul, but I'm a priest-scholar. Not a priest-scholar in a human sense, but in a spiritual sense. I have lived many past lives with the role of priest-scholar. If you do some due diligence and search the Internet for the *Michael Teachings*, you will learn about soul levels and roles.

* * * *

Note: I have included a short *Michael Teachings* overview in Appendix Two.

* * * *

There are five soul levels and seven roles. Everyone has a soul level and a role. If you read the *Michael Teachings*, you should be able to approximately guess yours. Many people have a role and sub-role. I have a sub-role of scholar. That means I have spent many lifetimes studying spirituality. You could say I have a Ph.D. in soul spirituality.

Now that you know that humanity has been blind to the truth, you can understand why our problems are so overwhelming.

All we are doing is compounding them because we have no clue how to fix them. This is why both sides of this political cold war are doomed to failure. They will be holding on tightly to their misguided beliefs trying the same thing over and over, while others begin to grasp the truth—that separation is a lie. There is only one truth, which is that we are all one.

So, if we are all one, then our political and cultural systems must adhere to that truth. Otherwise, they are a lie and will break down.

Let's discuss the liberal narrative of racial injustice and why current solutions are misplaced. CRT (Critical Race Theory) is based on the idea that white people have created a racial hierarchy and are unconsciously or insidiously maintaining that hierarchy. It's a misplaced idea, and in fact, indoctrinates the idea that racism is ingrained into society. Thus, CRT actually reinforces the idea. It does not allow people to see each other as equals.

CRT also instills the idea that we are separate from each other, with each race being treated differently. Our differences become heightened and prevent integration. Ironically, CRT and wokeness have proliferated the magnifying glass on our differences. The stereotype of discrimination against black Americans is constantly shoved in our face in movies and television shows. Conversely, the stereotype of white privilege is also constantly on display.

The liberals are pushing these narrative stereotypes in their political war. This isn't all happening by accident. They are putting pressure on Hollywood and corporations to accept these stereotypes. We are seeing it also in the LGBTQ movement, where differences, again, are pushed into the spotlight. The more you push differences, the more you ingrain them. You get the opposite of what you intend.

War creates more war. Hate creates more hate. Separation creates more separation. Differences create more differences.

Chapter Three: Their Narratives

Conflict creates more conflict. Fear creates more fear. The only thing that brings us together is love. John Lennon had it right. Instead of pushing an agenda that attempts to change others, we should only try to change ourselves.

If you love yourself and those around you, that is the only catalyst you need. Amazingly, love is actually biological. You can literally heal yourself by loving yourself. Why? Because of the soul. The soul is energy and can pull in additional energy. Energy balances the body. All of our organs are vibrating at a certain frequency. Love works to keep our organs and frequencies in balance.

Sex is also useful to balance our soul energy and is one of the healthiest things we can do to the body. It works when two souls exchange energy during sex. Have you ever wondered about the purpose of a female orgasm? It is used to rebalance the body's soul energy. It's not just endorphins that make you feel good after sex, but also the rebalancing of the body's energy system. Thus, sex is not only for making babies. It's also for our health.

Love emits laughter, joy, and harmony. If you stay in a loving mindset, you evoke a catalyst of physical, mental, and emotional health. Conversely, if you hate, fear, and judge others, you do not evoke that catalyst of health. So, if you want to be healthy, love yourself, love others, and make love.

When you focus on other people (e.g., those people are socialists!) and not on solutions, you are not evoking love. And the only way we find solutions is to focus on the love of humanity and the love for each other.

The conservative's narrative that anyone can achieve the American Dream by working hard is toxic. It simply isn't true, and we all know it isn't true. Opportunity is not equally distributed in America. That narrative is not a solution. It is cold and lacks love.

At a certain point in the near future, many of the conservative narratives will break down because they do not offer solutions. Their narratives lack solutions because they lack love. They are not inclusive.

The irony of this political cold war is that many of the underlying narratives are totally bogus. The leftist-progressives prefer to focus on racism (white supremacy) instead of social class differences. Is the real problem racism or a class-based society, whereby the lower class is disenfranchised? The same social inequity and financial inequity that blacks face is felt by the poor. There are not a lot of differences between a poor white person and a poor black person. They both face huge struggles. Is this struggle really against white people, or is it against affluent people who refuse to let go of the Goldwater–Reagan agenda?

The same discrimination that blacks felt prior to 1964 is still felt today in America by the disenfranchised. Whereas black America received the Civil Rights Act of 1964, the disenfranchised remained trapped in a political agenda that doesn't care about them. That agenda is largely the Goldwater–Reagan conservative agenda of meritocracy. Success is largely defined by the lane you are born into, with a slight chance that you will get to change lanes into upward mobility. The conservatives want to prevent that mobility because they are afraid that if it is changed, their life of privilege will become threatened.

The affluent have an advantage over the rest of society. It just so happens that white people were the early settlers of America. They had a head start that people of color did not. However, expecting conservatives to acknowledge that this wasn't fair and to reshape society in a more equitable manner is quite an expectation. Amazingly, that is a big part of the political cold war, and something the liberals want to accomplish.

Chapter Three: Their Narratives

The imbalance of affluence between races is quite apparent, and black people were neglected quite vociferously in the past, including during slavery. Black people were not even allowed to stay in certain hotels or eat in certain restaurants until the 1960s. That wasn't that long ago. Now they hold political power in many large urban cities, and the black caucus has grown into a powerful force in Washington. We even elected a black man to be president. You would think this is significant progress. But the liberals are adamant that we have made very little progress with regard to social equity.

The anger of the liberals toward the conservatives is similar to the anger of the black community for being discriminated against. The BLM movement was a natural convergence of both groups. The irony is that anger will not solve their issues. A few days ago, President Biden called *Fox News* one of the most destructive forces in America today. Clearly, that is an angry assertion. He insinuated that it was harmful to America and should be reformed in some manner to help America create a better future.

Where does that anger come from? Does he really believe that those who watch *Fox News* are destructive elements of society? And since *Fox News* is perhaps the single most purveyor of Republican values, is he implying that the Republican Party is a destructive element of society? The answer is clearly yes, and it is symptomatic of this political cold war.

While the liberals are angry at conservatives and want to see them lose all vestiges of political power and societal influence, the same can be said of conservatives. They have almost become mirror images of each other from a distaste standpoint. These are two enemies who do not like each other. This type of vitriol in American politics did not exist until the Bernie Sanders campaign in 2016, which lit the fuse.

Why doesn't either side in this political cold war see issues from the other's point of view? Because we are past that point in history. There is no going back. The war has begun, and those who are fighting the war have taken up sides. Now they will fight until there is a winner.

Ironically, this is a stealth war, and most people are either unaware that it is occurring or are in denial that it is taking place. In fact, many people will argue that it isn't taking place at all and is just politics as usual. That's baloney. I've followed politics closely since 1980, and something clearly changed in 2016.

I have found that conservatives are more apt to agree that a political cold war is taking place, but most of them are in denial that the liberals have a reason to be fighting against them. Instead, they just consider liberals to be insane or socialists/communists who want to destroy the country. In other words, conservatives don't understand why the conservative platform could be the wrath of liberals. Or, why that wrath could possibly have any merit.

I have tried to get liberals to admit that the goal of this war is to stealthily bypass the Constitution in its current form and instill a new form of government. That is not something they want to talk about publicly. Why? Not because they don't agree with the premise, but because they know that it will give their enemy a political issue to fight with (when you are in a war, you never help your enemy).

Liberals are fine with espousing the weaknesses and degradations of conservatives, but admitting that a war is taking place is tantamount to saying a revolution is occurring. They don't want to go there because it gives their enemy something to fight against. They much prefer a more subtle, stealth approach.

Ironically, the MSM is helping them with this goal/tactic. Everything I have written is true, yet the MSM does not cover this

Chapter Three: Their Narratives

story. Now, why is that? Isn't it obvious? The MSM has made a strategic decision to change the country and help the liberals to achieve their goals. If it wasn't so blatant, you would call me a conspiracy theorist. But it is blatant, and thus nefarious.

Yes, I am implying, and accurately so, that the MSM is part of the political cold war and has taken sides. Thus, a stealth revolution is taking place. However, as I said previously, neither side can win. And since neither side can win, the MSM is destroying itself, which is clear to see for those paying attention.

The conservatives think they can simply control the Senate and the Supreme Court to maintain their way of life. Or, more ambitiously, control the presidency, Congress, and the Supreme Court to maintain their way of life. They are not interested in helping the liberals with their issues, because they don't see those issues as problems.

The conservatives see their responsibility of maintaining the greatest nation on Earth. It doesn't need to be fixed. It needs to be maintained. We just have to stick to what we already know and what we do best. This is the Goldwater–Reagan agenda, as espoused by the Republican Party platform. Not much has changed in America since Reagan instilled the foundation of that platform in the 1980s after he learned most of it from Goldwater.

The Reagan-Goldwater agenda is a naïve approach to politics. It is an approach that breeds anger and contempt and ultimately unleashed a political cold war. One thing that it has fostered is a plethora of Americans who are disenfranchised, stuck in their lane of poverty or lack. The affluent conservatives have had no motivation to create some type of social and financial equity. Instead, they have watched from the sidelines as poverty has flourished in large urban areas.

As this poverty has proliferated, so has crime. And this crime does not always remain in impoverished areas. While most of the murders in America have been predominantly in the lower-class areas, crime is beginning to proliferate into all neighborhoods. This is what happens when you ignore a problem. It festers and erupts into a conflagration.

Once society devolves, crime becomes ubiquitous. It steadily removes the quality of life that once existed. In some third-world countries, police officers wear military gear and hold machine guns. We have almost fallen to that level. Yet, conservatives refuse to acknowledge that it is a problem they need to solve. Instead, they call for more funding of the police.

I don't think we have a racism problem in America. I think we have a class problem. The middle class is shrinking, and the lower class is being ignored. Conservatives believe that any attempts at fixing this problem (if it is even a problem) will make the problem worse. They see attempts by the government to fix social equity as having zero possibility of succeeding.

From this obstinate stubbornness on the part of conservatives to deal with social and financial inequity, the leftist-socialist movement emerged. Their anger took years to build and solidify. They are no longer in the mood to negotiate. They are in this to win and will do whatever it takes. Ironically, they don't care if it destroys the country. In fact, the heart of their objective is to create a new country with a new face.

From their standpoint, the first thing you have to do is win the political cold war. Unless you win, no change can occur. This is why we are seeing such insanity from the liberals (voting without IDs, an open border with Mexico, vax and mask mandates, a 49 miles per gallon federal guideline by 2026, defund the police initiatives, attempts to tax corporations at high rates, attempts to tax unrealized gains, etc.). They don't care about the ramifications. What's

Chapter Three: Their Narratives

important is taking over government, and that is accomplished by dramatically changing America's values.

It should be noted that if the Senate currently had 60 democratic senators that we likely would have a wealth tax on unrealized gains. In theory, this sounds like an attractive way of creating a fairer tax system and more equitable society. The super-rich have a disproportionate amount of wealth, so let's take their wealth (via a wealth tax) and spread it around using government programs. However, it will have the opposite effect. It will reduce the incentive for the rich to invest, because more wealth just means more taxes. The way to generate wealth and equity is not to tax wealth. But the liberals do not care about logic and economics. They want equity, even if that means damaging the economy.

UBI (universal basic income) is another liberal economic favorite that will have bad consequences on the economy. Today, UBI is being tested in some cities on a small scale, and is currently only an idea on the national level. UBI is an extension of existing government programs that provide assistance to the needy. It is also equated with generating more equity in society. Basically, it is helicopter money (the concept that Fed Chairmen Ben Bernanke made famous by saying they could throw money from helicopters to the public), and is similar to never-ending stimulus checks.

UBI sounds good in practice, but it would have a bad outcome. UBI has two problems. First, the money has to come from somewhere. Inevitably, with today's norm of large budget deficits, it would come from adding more national debt. At what point do we go bankrupt? Second, it creates a disincentive for people to work. How many of you remember that people would not go back to work when they were still receiving COVID stimulus checks?

Let's end this chapter by listing some of the liberal narratives. Amazingly, many of them are new. This newness has injected a sense of revolutionary zeal into the liberal agenda. It has also been quite shocking to the country and the conservatives.

Many of these narratives strike at the heart of how the liberals want to redefine America. Let's list some of them. 1) Higher taxes for the affluent and corporations. 2) Support for green energy and a move away from carbon-based energy. 3) Free childcare. 4) Free college. 5) Paid extended maternity leave. 6) Healthcare subsidies to the less affluent. 7) Censored speech on social media. 8) Support for LGBTQ rights. 9) Support of pay equity. 10) Support for illegal immigrants. 11) Support for vaccine mandates. 12) Support for increased business regulations. 13) Support for unions. 14) Support for CRT taught in schools. 15) Support for voting rights legislation that does not require an ID to vote. 16) Support for increasing the minimum wage. 17) Support of gun control. 18) Support of abortion rights. 19) Support for college debt forgiveness. 20) Support for government expansion.

All of these are narratives that *CNN* and *MSNBC* proudly support and expound upon daily. As do the major networks and print media, just not as vociferously. It is a kumbaya agreement by the media that the liberal platform is what America needs. You will not hear any attacks on these narratives unless you wander over to a conservative media outlet.

Is this simpatico relationship between liberal politicians and the MSM healthy for America? No, it is not. What is unfolding is an attack on individual freedom as the liberal agenda gets pushed to the forefront without adequate debate by the public, or scrutiny by the media. The narratives drown out any dissent. In fact, since this is a war, the dissent is now considered disinformation. This is becoming more and more common. A good example is how the media supported the vaccine mandates, even though it was an experimental vaccine with very little testing.

Chapter Three: Their Narratives

Another thing that is dangerous when the media begins expounding political narratives is that it is a slippery slope of parroting propaganda that are falsehoods – lies. It is ironic that liberals seem to have an obsession with misinformation yet seem to be masters of it. They have to be, because they are trying to pull the wool over our eyes by stealthily reshaping our values.

They constantly say they support Democracy. This is a big lie. They say that because they know the ultimate way to achieve their goals is via controlling government, and that can only be done at the ballot box. Democracy is their Achilles heel. What they really want is power. If they can subvert Democracy to achieve power, then they will.

Neither party supports Democracy. Both parties no longer care about the will of the people unless it suits their agenda. If they supported Democracy, then they would pay attention to polls. And neither party do.

Clearly, the majority of Americans support restricting illegal immigration. Do the liberals care? Absolutely not. As I just mentioned, they only care about polls if it suits their agenda. The liberals, with the MSM's help, are pushing agendas that are clearly not popular with the majority of Americans. This leads liberals to attempt to control the narratives and dissent. It's a very dangerous path for America, but one we are currently on.

While *Fox News* is not leading America to a better future, at least it is there to call out some of this liberal propaganda from the MSM. We are currently in a war of narratives, and most of them are misleading at best, and flat-out lies at worst.

Chapter Four

TRUMP & SANDERS

Donald Trump was the first conservative president since Ronald Reagan. Both Bush administrations were not far-right and governed with moderate ideologies. What Reagan put in motion during the 1980s was the birth of the modern conservative movement. It was also probably the birth of the modern leftist-socialist movement as a counter to Reagan's conservativism, although it took time to manifest into a national movement.

To say that Trump was a lightning rod of controversy for liberals is an understatement. They were in no mood for a conservative president. They labeled him as a racist; white supremacist; misogynist; bigot; and all-in-all, an immoral, detestable human being.

Trump carried a lot of baggage from past behavior and past statements. When you combined that with becoming the leader of the conservative movement, that was just too much to bear for liberals. They made it their agenda from day one of his presidency to discredit him and, if possible, push him out of office for being unfit to serve.

Trump was actually impeached twice by the House of Representatives, and it seemed like he was under investigation during his entire term in office. The liberals detested him from his first day in office and never let up.

Ironically, he was embraced with almost the same enthusiasm as Reagan by the conservatives. He was almost universally loved by the conservatives, who were excited to have the Reagan agenda back in play.

Trump ran as a populist, but that was a façade to get elected. His true colors shone through once in office. His ideology was clearly in alignment with the Republican Party, which had skewed to the right. He did not care about the middle class or lower class, in the same vein as Reagan. What mattered to him once in office was supporting the platform of the Republican Party.

During Trump's first campaign he boldly implied he would go against the Republican platform of globalism (free trade) and bring back manufacturing jobs. This could have been easily accomplished by requiring companies who import products into America to make a percentage here. If large corporations would have been required to make some of their products in the US, the middle class and lower class would have been benefited big-time. It would have been the type of populism he promised. Instead, we got a half-hearted attempt to re-write NAFTA.

That platform has already been outlined, but I'll repeat it here.

1) God. Supporting Christian values of the nuclear family and morality. This led to the rejection of abortion and LGBTQ rights.

2) Patriotism. Valuing the history of America, especially its military successes. This led to support of the military and its agenda of keeping America strong globally.

3) Business. The objective of keeping taxes and regulations low, so that businesses can thrive and achieve the American Dream. A pro-business, free market, capitalist economy is considered a necessity for America's stability and success.

4) Immigration. Ensuring immigration laws are enforced, and that border security is sufficient.

5) Limited government. Controlling the size of government and its influence.

6) Individualism. Ensuring that personal liberties are not infringed.

7) Gun rights. Support the 2nd amendment and ensure it is not infringed.

8) Rule of law. Support for government agencies that enforce existing laws.

9) Free speech. Support for the legal right to voice one's opinion.

10) Fiscal responsibility. Support for fiscal restraint and mindfulness of the risk of large budget deficits for future generations.

If you read between the lines, liberals are against this entire platform. As the liberals have gained more influence, especially with the MSM, they have vocally opposed this platform.

Trump was entering an incendiary caldron of vitriol against the conservative agenda. The liberals were ready to implement their agenda (described below) and were adamant of not allowing the country to veer right. The Republican platform was not acceptable in their mind.

The constant attack of Trump by the MSM and liberals was more of an attack on conservative values than on Trump himself. Sure, Trump has some personality traits that are morally questionable, but most billionaires are not angels. The ego and motivation required to become a billionaire can lead to questionable behavior. As the saying goes, power corrupts. And if there is one thing billionaires acquire, it is power.

So, the combination of Trump's personal behavior and the Republican platform was too much for the liberals to accept. They attacked Trump relentlessly, but what they were really doing was beginning the political cold war that has now unfolded. They decided to go to war against Trump, which we lived through from 2016 to 2020. *CNN* and *MSNBC* almost dedicated their programming to Trump-bashing for four years. Again, what they were really doing was attacking the conservative agenda. They used Trump's personality imperfections as a cover.

This might not be apparent, but this fight by the liberals to destroy the conservative agenda is even more fervent than the fight for civil rights in the early 1960s. We don't see many protests, other than those by BLM or those who protest police injustice, but the fight is being fought mostly through the media and by liberal politicians.

Trump was the perfect target for the liberals. He is deeply flawed and had no intention of helping the liberals, middle class, or lower class. His agenda was clear early on in his presidency that he would toe the line with the Republican platform. His slogan was Make America Great Again (MAGA). But this was misleading. It really meant that his objective was to maintain the existing class structure, thereby allowing the affluent to remain affluent, as well as to make more people affluent. It's like George Carlin told us: they call it the American Dream because you have to be asleep to believe it.

Once Trump appeared on the scene, the liberals had already begun to assemble. In fact, it was during his 2016 campaign that Bernie Sanders began his quest to reshape the country. The leftist-socialists had been on the rise during the eight years of the Obama administration, but had not found its voice or agenda. Bernie gave them both.

Once Bernie gave them direction, Trump had zero chance of calming the storm. That storm raged during Trump's four years in office and continues to rage today. The war has even intensified since Trump left office. Now the leftist-socialists want to instill their values onto the country. They are eager and passionate to succeed, no matter if they have to destroy the very fabric of society and create a new way of life.

Chapter Four: Trump & Sanders

The conservatives created the foundation of modern America from 1980 until 1992. That foundation is still in place. If your read between the lines of the Republican platform listed above, you will find that this platform is largely still in place. The platform of the liberals, which I'm about to outline, is still a dream of the leftist-socialists, and an affront to the current values that conservatives hold dearly. To them, the conservative agenda is the very fabric of America going back to the founding of the country.

If you noticed, the number one item that I listed on the Republican platform was God and Christian values. This polarizes the Republicans even further by instilling their religious beliefs into politics.

Many would argue that America was founded on the separation of Church and State, and that this separation is an integral part of why America has been successful. However, many Republicans would argue that without Christian values guiding our laws that we are lost. In some respects, this foundation of the Republican Party is largely unspoken until an elected official brings it up in a public platform, which is actually quite common.

Is religion (Christianity) in politics a problem? The left would probably say yes, but it has largely been a non-factor in how our laws are written. Albeit, there are exceptions, such as LGBTQ and abortion laws.

Okay, let me list the general platform of the liberals.

1) Government is necessary. Use government programs for the betterment of humanity.

2) Human rights are the responsibility of the government. Create laws to ensure that all humans are treated fairly and justly.

3) Equity is the responsibility of the government. Create laws to ensure that all humans have equal opportunity and equal treatment. It also includes making more equitable tax laws.

4) Worker rights are the responsibility of the government. Create laws to protect worker rights.

5) The environment is the responsibility of the government. Create laws to ensure the environment is not harmed and is improved when harm is identified.

6) Children are the responsibility of the government. This encompasses creating school curricula that best serve their needs and providing government agencies to protect their rights. It also includes laws to support maternity leave and childcare.

7) The poor and disenfranchised are the responsibility of the government. This encompasses creating laws and government programs to help people in need.

8) Gun control. Restrict access to deadly guns to create a safer America.

9) Support for abortion rights. Ensure access for abortions.

10) Support for voting rights legislation that does not require an ID to vote.

When you compare this platform with the Republicans, you can see that the chasm that has opened between the parties was inevitable. And as extreme elements in both parties have come to dominate the political debate, the political cold war was inevitable.

I don't know the exact moment when the liberals got their voice in America, but I think it was during the 2016 presidential race. Once Trump won, they were ready to fight. The vitriol was intense, and it has never abated ever since.

It is clear that the liberals will never again accept a conservative as their president. Conversely, it is clear that the conservatives will never accept a liberal as their president. The battle lines have been drawn, and now we fight. In fact, the war has clearly already begun.

Again, there will be no winner. Each side can try to muster a political majority to implement their agendas, but neither agenda

Chapter Four: Trump & Sanders

is tenable as a solution. Both can only have ugly outcomes that will result in failure.

The human soul only knows two things: love and sovereignty. Love is our core, and freedom is our natural state. The Creator gives us free will, and that is the basis of freedom as our natural state.

So, the only culture that will have longevity is one where humans are given freedom. Government must be small, because once you give it too much power, it will usurp freedom. For humans to love each other, you have to create a society where equity and fairness reign. Now, how do you that without a strong government? Simple, you create a constitution that ensures peace and harmony. You are thinking that is impossible, but have you read my new constitution?

We can and will start over as a civilization. We will do exactly what I have done, which is to write a new constitution that solves all of our existing problems. Our Constitution was written before the industrial revolution or modern technology. It was written before capitalism existed. It was written for simpler times and, in fact, flourished for many decades. But its time has come to an end, and this will soon become apparent. In fact, if you are paying attention, you will see that we have been ignoring the Constitution for quite some time now. The conservatives ripped it up after 9/11, with their Patriot Act. And the liberals consider it a badge of honor to ignore it by steadily repealing free speech and gun rights.

It's not quite time yet to start over with a new constitution. The reason being that both sides still think they have a solution. We need to reach a point where both sides realize they don't have the answers. That time is coming. Second, we need a bit more time to awaken spiritually. We need to find an affinity with one another. That, too, is coming.

Bernie gave people hope. Ironically, that was Barrack Obama's slogan when he ran in 2008. Bernie started a revolution, and that revolution has not burned out yet. It needs more time before it is ready to fade away.

It is ironic that Bernie transformed the Democratic Party, and yet not one of his campaign platform issues was included in the 2020 Democratic Platform. Here is a snapshot of Bernie's platform:

1) Free community college
2) Cancel student debt
3) Expand Social Security
4) Eliminate homelessness via a housing for all initiative
5) Universal childcare
6) Eliminate medical debt
7) Medicare for all
8) The Green New Deal

    a. 100% renewable energy for electricity and transportation by 2030.

    b. Build renewable energy generation capacity (publicly owned).

    c. Build a smart grid (publicly owned).

    d. Phase-out non-sustainable energy sources.

    e. Regulate greenhouse gases.

It's easy to see why these were not part of the 2020 Democratic platform. They are all expensive programs, and each one requires enormous political capital to get passed. Regardless if these issues are not part of the platform, they are on the minds of the leftist-socialists. They want to see the majority of these issues turned into law.

The Biden Administration seems content with focusing on equity issues and the rights of the oppressed. They have singled out the rich in their budgets, with Biden's campaign promise of raising taxes on those who make more than $400,000 in income. Plus, they have ostracized large corporations for taking advantage of U.S. citizens during this high inflationary period. Recently, Nancy Pelosi, the Speaker of the House, recommended price controls on gasoline. She said it was unfair that large oil companies were making high profits because of inflation and the war in Ukraine.

Product price control is another philosophical divergence between conservatives and liberals. The liberals have no qualm using the government for the benefit of the whole, even if it harms the efficiency of the economy. Conversely, the conservatives are more pro-business and are loathe and reticent to take measures that will harm the economy.

The current Democratic platform is quite restrained and mimics the Obama era. They want to raise the minimum wage, protect women's rights, protect LGBTQ rights, expand access to long-term care, expand access to substance abuse programs, promote workers' rights, reform the tax code to make it more equitable, protect consumer rights, protect the environment, protect voting rights, provide relief to student debt, and end gun violence.

While the Democratic platform is restrained, don't let that fool you. Their real agenda is much more subtle and aggressive. Not only do they want to pass Bernie's platform, but they want to change the very soul of America. They want to change America's values from a meritocracy based on individualism, to one based on government power and collectivism. This change to the soul of America is what this political cold war is all about.

Recently, Elon Musk made an offer to acquire Twitter. His offer was accepted, but the deal has not closed, and the Biden Administration is keen on finding a way to kill it. Musk is aware of this new leftist-socialist agenda and has decided to pick a side and fight against it. The combination of Twitter and Facebook instituting harsh censorship on their platforms is part of this change to the soul of America.

I will be discussing this more in depth in the chapter on free speech. I'm mentioning it here to show how the move to the left by the Democratic Party, and the leftist-socialist movement, is much more aggressive than the bland Democratic platform.

The large social media companies are controlling the political narratives in the public arena, and this is creating a foundation upon which the liberals can build. Once the narratives are controlled, then the people are controlled. From there, it's not a stretch to imagine them obtaining political power. Then once they control all three branches of government, they can swoop in and pass not only Bernie's platform but even a harsher platform of collectivism.

If this occurs, their leftist-socialist agenda will surely fail, as dystopian outcomes push people to rebel. You can't create societal harmony or business vibrancy using collectivist government control. We've watched that outcome in Cuba, Venezuela, and North Korea. They think the Chinese have been able to do it fairly well, but they ignore the fact that capitalism is a major factor generating their economic success, and they have a single political party that has absolute control.

Bernie is about as far left as you can go. The liberals have adopted his ideas and platform. There is no going back for them. In fact, they have taken it a step further. Now they want to re-write the Constitution (by using new laws written by Congress and approved by the Supreme Court) and re-create America. They want a new America.

This possible new America is what the conservatives are fighting against. So, you have two well-entrenched parties fighting to win.

But this is more than just a political squabble; it is for the very soul of America.

Unfortunately for them, neither side can win. The conservatives can kick the can down the road for a few more years until America begins to implode into a dystopian mess, where crime becomes ubiquitous; government agencies lose all sense of efficiency; and the economy muddles along, gasping for air. But the can only has a few more kicks left in it, until society gives up on its system of individualism and merit-based achievement.

Conversely, the liberals are living in dreamland if they think their agenda has any chance of success. You can't remove and squeeze freedom and expect any type of harmony. Isn't it obvious what types of outcomes we get when the government is involved? Look at the inner-city, large urban school districts. They are an utter failure, and government has had zero success at fixing them. In fact, all they have done is make it worse. It's gotten so bad that liberals want to stop giving out report cards with grades. Everybody passes. Everybody graduates, but nobody learns anything. Welcome to stage one of dystopia.

In addition to the failure of large urban school districts, look at the crime and murder rates in these cities. They are already approaching dystopian levels, and we haven't even reached the point where the liberals are in charge and implementing the leftist-socialist platform, whereby business growth stagnates. What will happen when unemployment rates double in these areas? Will the government have answers? No chance.

So, as I have pointed out, both sides can't win the war they are so intent on fighting. The American political cold war is a zero sum game.

Chapter Five

MMT and Economics

MMT stands for Modern Monetary Theory. It is the economic theory invented by Japan in the early 1990s after their economic bubble popped in 1989. Instead of allowing their banks and corporations to fail, the Japanese did something unprecedented: they digitally printed an enormous amount of money and bailed them out, regardless if the company was solvent or could remain solvent. Plus, they lowered interest rates to extremely low levels for the entire decade. They even used negative rates, which was unprecedented.

After the Japanese central bank bailed out insolvent banks and corporations, they proceeded to use two tools to keep the economy from faltering. The first was to continuously stimulate the economy by expanding the money supply via digital money printing. Their preference for stimulating during the first half of the 1990s was to use infrastructure projects. They did several of these, but none of them created much economic growth, although they did seem to prevent any deep recessions.

Another thing they used to stimulate the economy was to buy stocks using printed digital money. Today, the Japanese central bank owns more than 80% of the exchange-traded funds (ETFs) that trade in Japan! The United States Federal Reserve central bank (Fed) hasn't started buying stocks yet, but you can bet they will. They have been a good student of Japanese MMT.

The second tool was to artificially keep interest rates low. This was accomplished by the Japanese central bank purchasing Japanese government bonds. The Japanese central bank owns so many Japanese government bonds that some of them no longer trade on a daily basis. Why? Because nobody has any to sell except the Japanese central bank! This is what MMT has created. A big economic mess.

It got so bad that Japan had to use yield curve control (YCC) to keep rates at artificially low levels. At one point, the Japanese central bank fixed their 10-year bond at zero percent. How? They guaranteed that they would purchase any 10-year bonds that traded above zero percent. This left investors with the only option of buying 10-year bonds with zero percent yield or negative yields. In fact, it was quite common to see these bonds trade with negative yields.

Note that the Fed hasn't started using YCC yet, at least not publicly, but you can bet they have discussed it and probably will at some point. High interest rates are very dangerous once you begin using MMT. I'll explain why shortly.

The Japanese central bank buys most of their country's government-issued bonds because investors don't want bonds that have a zero percent or negative yield. They have also purchased many of the stock market ETFs that investors thought were too risky or overvalued.

In effect, the Japanese central bank started managing their economy in a proactive way, beginning in 1989. This was effective at preventing recessions, but conversely, not very good at generating economic growth. Since they began MMT in 1989, they have had perhaps the slowest growing economy of any advanced country. Moreover, they destroyed their free market, which likely prevented their economy from growing. They have had sluggish growth ever since MMT was adopted, and they call the 1990s the lost decade because of their poor economic performance.

Chapter Five: MMT and Economics

Why am I writing about economics in a book on politics? Well, America is and has always been about business and money. It's not a misconception to call America one big corporation. In fact, America invented the corporation with the robber barons (Rockefeller, Carnegie, Mellon, Morgan, etc.). Politics and economics go hand in hand in America. And today, MMT is at the heart of our economic system, and thus needs to be included in this book.

MMT is the belief that central banks can control economies by using money printing to inject liquidity as needed, along with interest rate control. If the economy slows down, then you simply inject more liquidity. Government debt becomes a secondary concern, and a minor one at that. The primary concern is liquidity. Under this theory, government debt can grow as large as needed and never needs to be paid back. In fact, proponents of this theory believe that government debt is not a problem and can grow to infinity.

This type of thinking was considered insane in America until 9/11 occurred in 2001. Until 9/11, government debt was considered a serious problem, and large government deficits were avoided. Throughout the 1990s, we made a serious effort to balance the budget precisely because of our concerns of acquiring too much government debt. After the run-up in government debt during the 1980s, it was considered prudent to return to our fiscal conservative ways. Prior to 1980, the government never had a debt problem, and a $100 billion deficit was an anomaly.

Then 9/11 occurred, and suddenly we changed our economic philosophy. Suddenly, debt no longer mattered. We started having trillion-dollar budget deficits, and our national debt exploded. How did that sudden change happen? Simple, we copied the Japanese! If they could have large government budget deficits, then so could we. If they could avoid economic pain by printing money, then we could, too.

MMT arrived in America when 9/11 occurred. It was utilized out of political expediency. We had just been attacked by terrorists (at least that is the narrative!), and we were not going to let that event bring down our economy. So, we printed money and injected liquidity, along with low interest rates. It worked, and shortly after, a housing boom ensued (or was it an artificial housing bubble?).

The American people had no say in this change in economic philosophy. It was all done by a few power players in Washington. No one at that time had the will to stand up and say it was a bad idea to expand the national debt and run high budget deficits. After all, we had just balanced the budget in 1999. Were our memories that short? You would have thought that at least a few politicians would have stood up and made a fuss. Instead, it was quickly agreed in Washington that adding debt and expanding the money supply was our best option to combat the recession that occurred after 9/11 in 2001.

Both parties agreed to this economic strategy. Ironically, the Republicans were in power. They were supposed to be the party of fiscal restraint. But it was a moderate Republican in office, George W. Bush. The conservatives could not stop him, and it was a very dangerous precedent that emerged.

So, MMT emerged in America. The Fed gladly supported the expansion of debt with lower interest rates to give MMT some bite. It was the beginning of the end of the free market in America. Artificial low interest rates and the injection of liquidity quickly became the new norm for our economic policy. The stock market rose, the economy rose, and the housing market boomed. It appeared to be a good decision, but looks can be deceiving. In truth, the free market would no longer be allowed to stand on its own, and the Great Financial Crisis (GFC) was looming a few years ahead, in 2008.

Chapter Five: MMT and Economics

* * * *

It should be noted that prior to MMT, the Fed's mandate was to control inflation and maximize employment. This mandate was focused more on helping people than on asset valuations, whereby the 1% own most of the wealth. That changed after MMT, although the Fed has never publicly stated that the mandate has changed.

Today, the Fed's unstated true mandate has become convoluted. In fact, I would submit the overriding mandate is financial stability. And because the stock market has become so important to the economy, it has now become a focal point of the Fed.

The point I want to make is that the Fed is now more concerned with asset valuations and corporate interests than helping the people. By focusing on financial stability, the people become a secondary consideration. In fact, you could say the Fed and Wall St. have become simpatico.

* * * *

The leftist-socialists were not around yet in 2001, but the Democrats had no problem with the decision to use large deficit spending after 9/11. After all, they were the party of big government. They were clapping at the idea of spending more money. That was their agenda.

Ironically, the Republicans ushered in MMT. It happened under George W. Bush's administration. They gave their blessing to ignoring government debt. In fact, after 9/11, there has never been a call to reduce the government debt by the Republican Party. Perhaps a few conservatives raised objections from time to time, but deficit reduction never made its way into the party platform.

The annual federal budget runs from September 30th to October 1st. So, 9/11 occurred right before the 2002 budget began, and it was already determined. So, in 2002, we didn't have the opportunity to do profligate spending, and the budget deficit was only $158 billion, which wasn't too bad. But then it jumped to $328 billion in 2003 (the first real budget after 9/11), and then $413 billion in 2004. Those were not recessionary years. That was MMT in action, and a signal of what was to come.

MMT destroys the free market, and a vibrant free market is part of the Republican platform. Ironically, economists have never been vocal about the damage MMT does to the free market. The reason why is because nobody wants to risk going back to a free-market economy. The risk of a financial crisis has been high since 9/11 and has only increased in risk as time passes. We have become so dependent on MMT and the Fed's manipulation of the economy that nobody has the courage to return to a free-market economy.

And the fear is legitimate. We can't go back. We have already destroyed the free market. Going back would not be easy and would be painful.

This is where politics comes into play. The economy is broken. Neither party can depend on it. The Republicans want to make America great again with a vibrant economy, where everyone is lifted up economically, but that is a fairytale. MMT will not allow that.

The liberals are quite happy that MMT is destroying capitalism. That is actually part of their platform, and the woke mob is not shy about articulating that fact. Many of them publicly excoriate capitalism. They want the government to be more involved in the regulation and control of the economy, and the more involvement, the better. In fact, if Joe Biden had the votes in 2021, he would have tried to pass legislation that would have vastly increased the government's involvement in the economy. He wanted to increase

Chapter Five: MMT and Economics

government oversight of business and legislate mandatory green energy programs and the reduction of fossil fuels. That would have been the path liberals wanted to follow in the future. He did not get the votes, but he came close.

It is quite clear that the liberal agenda with the economy is to increase the government's involvement. They want more regulations and control of powerful corporations, along with higher taxes. They also want to legislate how workers are treated, with more protection from discrimination, along with paid maternity leave. Allowing workers to unionize is also a big agenda item. Plus, they want more ways for government to maintain business oversight that has teeth (the ability to fine companies that do not adhere to government regulations).

I don't think it is hyperbole to say that liberals want to replace free-market capitalism with a new type of quasi-government control of the economy, with MMT as the foundation. It's ironic that the Republicans brought the monster of MMT to life.

What makes MMT so appealing to the liberals is that it gives them a blank check to expand government programs. Joe Biden attempted to have a budget of $5 trillion in his first year in office. And it would have passed if he had the votes.

So, using MMT, the liberals want to spend their way to a better America and ignore debt and budget deficits. After all, with MMT, debt can expand to infinity. The liberal's economic plan of spending their way to a better America is as much of a pipe dream as the conservative's plan of making America great again. Both parties have no path forward economically, not as long as MMT is in place, and I don't see that going away anytime soon.

MMT opens the door for a completely controlled economy. The Fed has already assumed a large role in the manipulation of the economy. The slippery slope of steady manipulation has already formed. It won't be long before the cryptocurrency "Fedcoin" appears, which will give them even more control of the economy. The Fedcoin will be a digital currency that exists in digital wallets that the Fed and the U.S. government can monitor. All of our dollars will likely need to be converted into digital money.

Our privacy will be evaporated once the Fedcoin appears. This is something the liberals look forward to and will embrace. Why? Their agenda is about the benefits of government control of society. They see it as the obverse of corporations and white men controlling society. They see government power as the only way to take power away from corporations and affluent white men.

Individualism and the free market (capitalism) go hand in hand. The liberals want to destroy both. And what better way than to destroy the free market and instigate more government control? MMT is a godsend for them. They can use unlimited amounts of debt to fund government programs. And if MMT does blow up and fail, then the government can come to the rescue. It's a win-win from their perspective.

The liberals want to eliminate individualism and replace it with collectivism. In tandem with this, they want to replace free-market capitalism with some form of a proactive Fed that utilizes MMT along with a powerful government that controls the economy. This would include price controls, wage controls, production controls, and high income taxes for the affluent.

The liberal agenda wants the government to decide how everyone lives and works. They assume that this type of collectivist culture will create harmony because the government knows what's best for society and humanity. This may sound like hyperbole, but it is exactly what the liberals want to achieve by winning this political cold war.

Chapter Five: MMT and Economics

The liberals want to extend regulations on business so that the government can have complete control over how businesses operate. For example, in the same way that they want to determine how and what children are taught in schools, they want to determine how businesses operate. They think if they win the political cold war, the government will get to dictate how we live all aspects of our lives.

If you think this is hyperbole, they already want to emulate the social score system that is in place in China. This social score system will include everything from what we purchase, what we do for entertainment, what we eat, our work performance, our social habits, etc. It is Orwell's book, *1984*, come to life.

In China today, if you have a low social score, you can't travel. Can you imagine that coming to America? Don't worry; it's not. I'm only pointing out what could happen if they win. Luckily, they can't, which I will be explaining why shortly. I only mention the social score because it is part of their agenda and part of the political cold war.

The political cold war is being fought on many economic fronts. You have the minimum wage, which the liberals want to be a living wage. The conservatives are fighting to keep the minimum wage low. Both positions are misplaced. The liberals should be fighting to shrink the number of pay scales, which is how you increase pay equity and increase pay at the lower end. The conservatives are misguided when they think that society will function efficiently by keeping a lower class disenfranchised and poorly paid.

Another huge issue is business regulations, which have a big impact on the economy. These regulations can range from environmental protection, safety, consumer protection, criminal oversight, record keeping, building codes, permitting, etc. There are many others that I can't think of. The government is constantly making it more difficult for businesses to operate. The liberals think this is a good thing and want to add more regulations. Conversely, the conservatives want to remove many existing regulations.

If the liberals have their way, we won't be able to grow food in our backyard, because that can only be done on a regulated farm. If you think I am out of my mind, this has already been advocated by liberals in Australia.

The problem with too many business regulations is that it does not allow the free market to operate efficiently. The more restrictions that are added, the less the market can operate efficiently. This is a big philosophical difference between the parties, with the liberals oblivious to the importance of market dynamics. Regardless, it is too late anyway for the conservatives to maintain a free market. It is already broken because of MMT.

The Fed injected trillions of printed digital dollars into the market after 2008 to ensure that another financial crisis did not occur. This had the effect of keeping asset prices up, but real growth in the economy was languid at best. In fact, the middle class and lower class continued to lose ground as their standard of living declined. All that money printing did was benefit the top 1%. Moreover, it further damaged the free market by mispricing assets using artificially low interest rates.

The conservatives have been in denial since 9/11 and the GFC. They pretended to believe that the economy is fine and remains the number one economy in the world. When Donald Trump was in office from 2016 to 2020, he routinely called it the greatest economy ever. Many conservatives actually believed him. In fact, the economy was only growing because of MMT (artificially low interest rates, large budget deficits, and Fed money printing). The budget deficits under Trump averaged nearly $2 trillion per year. He added $7.8 trillion to the national debt during his four years in office. Why do you need $2 trillion budget deficits when the economy is not in a recession or a war? MMT.

Chapter Five: MMT and Economics

What we have had since 9/11 was a Potemkin (fake) economy. It was propped up using MMT, and that's where we sit today. The liberals are fine with it and have no qualms of extending debt to infinity. The conservatives are starting to get nervous, but they only seem to complain about high budget deficits when a Democrat is the president.

The conservatives naively believe that the U.S. economy is so strong and resilient that all we need are low taxes and fewer regulations, and all will be fine. The living standards of the middle and lower class continue to retrench, but conservatives refuse to notice. They are wearing rose-colored glasses and living in a fairytale. It's similar to the band playing on the Titanic as the ship sinks.

Both parties are incredibly blind to the realities of the U.S. economy. It is dying, and neither seems to care. Well, that's not exactly true. The conservatives believe it will die if the liberals are allowed to add too many regulations and taxes. But they don't believe it will die if a conservative Republican is the president at the helm.

While America's social problems (fairness, equality, equity, and opportunity) are the heart of the problem, the economy is not that far behind in importance. The difference between them is that you can't fix our social problems by focusing on the economy. Conversely, if you fix the social problems, the economy will fix itself.

Conservatives like to focus on economic issues. Conversely, they loathe focusing on social issues. On social issues, they prefer to point fingers and pretend it's not their fault. A good example is crime. They will put up a list of crime statistics from inner-city urban areas that are run by Democrats and say it is all their fault. Amazingly, they actually believe it is the Democrat's fault and has nothing to do with them (the conservatives).

If the conservatives have their way, the economy will continue to operate as it does today, with the largest benefits going to the top 1%. What they don't see is that the clock is running out. America has been living off of debt for 40 years and is about to lose its credit (ability to borrow money).

It won't be much longer before the U.S. government is forced to partially default on its debt. My guess is we will pay 50 cents on the dollar to bondholders, and the Fed will lose its ability to print digital dollars at will. Once that happens, everything the conservatives believe about economics will be shattered.

The same will apply to the liberals, who will be forced to acknowledge that debt expansion is not their ticket to prosperity.

Chapter Six

Free Speech

This might be the biggest issue that undermines the liberals. They are adamant that free speech is too dangerous to allow. The irony is that the liberal MSM spreads information that is highly suspect. I'm not going to use examples, but anyone who thinks that the MSM has not become politically biased is naïve. I used to watch the liberal MSM cable networks. Sometime between 2016 to 2020, I stopped. Why? I simply no longer believed them. I wasn't alone; their viewership has declined. I think the main reason why is not because of the liberal ideology that they embrace, but the lack of believability of what is aired.

I would go so far as to say that journalism has died in America owing to the political bias that has become rampant. And if journalism is dead and all that we are reading is propaganda, then free speech becomes even more important.

A *New York Times* editorial writer recently wrote that free speech is an obsession with white men and is no longer appropriate in the modern era of mass communication. Basically, she implied that free speech is too powerful to allow. Indeed, it is powerful. This is why liberals want to control what you can read, say, or hear. Conversely, they do not want to allow public discourse on controversial topics. Those narratives are to be determined by the elites in government positions or by corporations who can control what information is released to the public. This type of control of information is very dangerous to freedom, but liberals think it is worth it if that is the only way to change a society that disgusts them.

The liberals began focusing on narratives shortly after Trump won in 2016, and those narratives have dominated the MSM. When the conservatives tried to fight back against these narratives, they were routinely banned from social media websites. Any conservative with more than 100,000 followers was destined to be banned. Why? Because the liberals were successful in getting the social media companies to agree with their narratives and to label conservatives' discourse as either misinformation or hate speech.

The ubiquitous banning of conservatives on social media platforms was really just flat-out censorship. The liberals simply didn't like the conservative values that were being discussed on public platforms. It was blatant discrimination against conservatives, although once COVID-19 appeared, the censorship extended to anyone who released COVID-19 information that was counter to the Biden Administration or CDC. The Biden Administration was very vocal about the importance of controlling this disinformation. Some posters received warnings, but most were simply banned for breaking their posting rules.

It became obvious early on in the Biden Administration that the large social media companies were being proactive in limiting both conservative discourse and COVID-19 information that ran counter to the Biden Administration or CDC. It felt chillingly similar to *Pravda*, the media arm of the old communist Soviet Union. The Biden Administration only wanted the narrative of the government to be discussed publicly, and all opinions and dissent were controlled.

Again, some of you are probably thinking I am once again slipping into hyperbole. But just this week, the Biden Administration announced a new group inside the DHS called the Disinformation Governance Board. Notice that this was not deployed at the Department of Justice, but instead at the DHS. This is more about fear and intimidation. The DHS is the internal military arm of the government. The Justice Department employees wear suits and comprise lawyers. The DHS wears military gear. People were calling this new group, the Ministry of Truth, as a parody on Orwell's book *1984*. But it very well could turn into something that is dystopic.

I should add that the person who was put in charge of this board is highly controversial and known for writing books about spreading misinformation that could be harmful to the public. She is known as someone who has liberal beliefs and thus is apt to have a bias of limiting free speech for the greater good. I think it is quite obvious that part of the agenda of this new agency is to give the government a tool that can be used to limit free speech.

This new group was formed one week after Elon Musk's offer to acquire Twitter. I don't think it was a coincidence. The White House press secretary said that misinformation would not be allowed in response to Musk's acquisition. This new misinformation group within DHS is likely the arm that will be used to enforce that objective.

Free speech is clearly under threat today. It's beginning to feel like a tyrannical government that no longer allows its citizens to share their opinions in public. That is already true to a certain extent. Just ask those people who have been banned from social media. But it feels like we have started down a slippery slope where discourse is steadily being squeezed into acceptable narratives. This is what Twitter's current CEO calls healthy speech.

* * * *

One of the most important beliefs that Christians hold is that God gave us free will. They got that one right. Christians have gotten most of the basic beliefs about God correct. They understand that God is loving and forgiving. Although, most Christians get wrong that God will judge our soul when we pass over to the other side after death. God does not judge. God can't because that wouldn't make any sense, because God is us. God does not judge life, and you will find that out when you pass to the other side. All you will feel is love, and zero judgment.

The core of the soul is love because that is the core foundation of God. It is similar to what a mother feels for her child. That type of love is unconditional. In fact, any love that is not unconditional is a lie. From unconditional love, freedom arises. This is where free will comes from.

So, our core is both love and freedom. Those two concepts are the soul's highest values. Life itself is about learning that truth.

So, when liberals claim that freedom of speech is dangerous, or try to curtail freedom of expression, they are going against the soul's highest value. They are swimming uphill, against nature. They are trying to fit a round peg into a square hole. It won't work. Life will always find a way to express its highest values.

The irony is that liberals think they are on the moral high ground by restricting unhealthy speech. In fact, they are creating a bigger problem with their misguided liberal ideology. When they prevent the free flow of ideas, they are caught in the dilemma of having to use lies and propaganda to rationalize censorship. They are trapped with trying to decide what is healthy for society. They have to become the Ministry of Truth, which is a political outcome, and has nothing to do with the truth. They are rationalizing that their own political ideas and beliefs are correct.

Liberals dislike libertarians because the latter demand their freedom and individualism. Libertarians want the government to stay out of their lives and leave them alone. They want the freedom

Chapter Six: Free Speech

and liberty to do what they want, and they especially want the freedom to voice their opinions.

To control libertarians and restrict their freedom and individualism, liberals have to control the narratives and information discourse of society. A free flow of information will protect libertarians and their freedom. That is a fact. Conversely, the best way to take away their freedom is via a political party (leftist-socialists) usurping power and relegating the Constitution to the dustbin. And if the liberals are going to rip up the Constitution, it is important that they control the narrative. Otherwise, they are going to have a revolution on their hands. And how do you control the narrative? You limit free speech.

We have been witnessing this control of information since 2016. For instance, cable news channels constantly propagate a narrative they want to push. One example is the idea that white supremacists are pervasive. President Biden says that the number one domestic terrorist threat is white supremacists, and then the cable news channels insinuate that alt-right conservatives are filled with these white supremacists. They say this over and over, and that conservatives are racists. It's not true. It's a narrative.

This is why on social media today, free speech is not only restricted, but vilified. And much of this vilified free speech is, in fact, true, although most of it is just opinions that liberals disagree with and consider dangerous or unhealthy for humanity.

For example, the public was not allowed to have a debate regarding the efficacy of the COVID-19 vaccines. The liberals decided that the vaccines were safe, and debate was cut off on social media. Those who tried to espouse opinions that the testing of the vaccine was inadequate were labeled as anti-science. Many of them lost access to their social media accounts.

It should be stated that these narratives are extremely potent in manipulating behavior. For instance, many doctors were fired from their jobs for simply stating their opinions regarding COVID-19 on social media. Anyone who dared to question the narrative publicly was ostracized by those who believed in it. Indeed, we live in a nation where our opinions have become a threat to our livelihood.

Freedom of expression, freedom of thought, and freedom of opinion are all now threatened by the liberal thought police. If you're not woke, and you work at a company that has a culture that leans liberal, then you are trapped in a work environment that discriminates against you. Thus, the liberals are re-creating what they are trying to prevent (discrimination). God does have a sense of humor.

The government vaccine narrative was very simple: the vaccines work and will save lives, and everyone should have them. Moreover, it had one objective, which was to get everyone vaccinated. The liberals believed in the narrative and wanted to pressure those who did not want to take the vaccine. Some liberals wanted to either prevent the unvaccinated from healthcare, or even round them up into detention centers. Polls showed many supported these positions. President Biden said that the COVID-19 policies and regulations were not about freedom, but about saving lives. This fits nicely with the liberal belief that the collective is more important than the individual.

Those who demanded the right to decide if they were vaccinated or not were vilified as troublemakers who were jeopardizing the safety of fellow Americans. This narrative was pushed by both the Administration and the MSM. It was more political than science. If the liberals had their way, a vaccine mandate from an executive order to require a COVID-19 vaccination for all Americans would have occurred. In fact, in Germany, they voted on a law to require all citizens over 60 to have the COVID-19 vaccination. Fortunately, it did not pass, but the vote was actually close and vigorously supported by the liberals in that country.

In Canada, the liberals were so strongly behind the COVID-19 vaccine mandates that they voted on a law to remove government pensions from anyone who was not vaccinated. That's just mean. It hasn't passed yet, but they are still trying.

Another thing that liberals vigorously supported with COVID-19 were vaccine passes. This was part of the political cold war as conservatives fought back against these mandates. We saw a plethora of these vaccine passes in blue states, and even quite a few in red states. But the conservatives fought hard against these mandates.

The most leftist-socialist countries, such as Australia, Canada, France, Germany, and Austria, all had harsh requirements for COVID-19 vaccine passes. America was on the verge of emulating some of these countries. California was perhaps the most anti-freedom with its COVID-19 mandates. New York and New Jersey weren't far behind.

The battle for individualism and freedom was fought over COVID-19 mandates. A big part of that battle was trying to share information, which was harshly controlled on social media. There was a huge outcry against a Joe Rogan interview on Spotify with a doctor who questioned the efficacy of the vaccines. The liberals tried in vain to get Joe Rogan fired for simply doing the interview.

Facebook, Twitter, and YouTube were all vigilant about preventing any false information regarding COVID-19 and the vaccinations. This was often blatant censorship, with the goal of following the CDC and administration narratives on COVID-19. Anyone who voiced opinions contrary to this narrative found their post deleted and potentially their account terminated.

This blatant censorship revealed the close relationship between liberal politicians and these large social media companies. It also revealed how the slippery slope of limiting free speech could easily morph into something that is skewed by a political agenda. For instance, those doing the censorship need to have direction. Someone has to decide what is censored. The social media companies can't do it completely on their own. They need some political input because the ramifications are too big, and new issues are constantly arising. For instance, with COVID-19, the narrative was set publicly in Washington. Then the social media companies tried to follow it. How will the narratives be set next time? Behind closed doors? Most likely.

Do you see how dangerous this can become? Twitter says that they use the determining factor of healthy speech. But what is that? Who gets to decide what is healthy? How do you keep politics or political beliefs from biasing your viewpoint? You can't! Moreover, Twitter, YouTube, and Facebook all have cultures that are left leaning. How does that impact how censorship is enforced? Can politics be kept out? Not likely.

I used COVID-19 as an example of how free speech is currently being controlled, but there are many topics that are censored on social media. Twitter, Facebook, and YouTube all use the concept of hate speech to censor what can be said or viewed. Here is a shortlist of topics that get heavily censored as hate speech because they are considered offensive to "some" people.

Abortion

Gun rights

LGBTQ rights

Immigration

Police funding

Videos of liberals expressing their beliefs

Chapter Six: Free Speech

- Videos of conservatives expressing their beliefs
- Vaccine mandates
- Vaccine efficacy
- BLM opinions
- Antifa opinions
- Crime opinions
- Homeless opinions
- Socialist opinions
- Alt-Right opinions
- January 6th opinions
- Homeopathic medicine
- Sex
- Criticism of the opposite sex
- Criticism of public officials

Of course, all of these topics can be discussed in a healthy way. The problem is that they can easily meander into areas that are considered unhealthy and upsetting to some groups. The liberals have become hypersensitive to discussing controversial issues. This is why conservative discourse is largely missing on Twitter and Facebook. Why? Because conservatives tend to speak their mind without a filter on most of these topics.

This list isn't close to being comprehensive. Once social media companies began censoring offensive material, nearly everything fits in that basket. Anyone who has been on one of these social media platforms for an extensive period of time knows how easy it is for people to get banned for trying to discuss some of these topics.

I can usually predict when someone will be banned, even when their opinion is harmless. Quite often, their infringement is that they told the truth. I often warn people when they begin espousing the truth that it is not allowed. I'll tweet a joke that they can't say that, and that the truth is not allowed. It might be a joke, but it is very close to how things work on the big social media platforms. The closer to the truth seems to be what raises red flags with the censor bots. It's easy to get over the target.

Once you begin censoring, you are left with only one outcome, which is the loss of freedom. Without freedom of speech, you can't have freedom. Why isn't this obvious to everyone? If society is not allowed to discuss and share what is on its collective mind, you are left with a banal interaction whereby the government, social media companies, and the MSM set the narrative of society. And that narrative inevitably leads to a very repressive culture where freedom and individualism are squashed.

The founding fathers knew the importance of freedom. That is why they said that all men (people) were created equal. It's true that they weren't ready yet to live that ideal, but they knew it was right, and that's why they wrote it down. Ironically, the liberals are still fighting for their freedom via equal rights, while simultaneously trying to take away the rights of others, via government control and censorship. How hypocritical is that? It's actually diabolical.

Liberals think that they can gain their freedom by giving the government more power (as long as they are the ones who hold the reins of power). It's total insanity. The soul was never meant to be smothered and controlled. It was meant to be free. Totally free.

What the liberals get wrong is that the collective can flourish with freedom. They think this is impossible. However, the concept, "if you love someone, set them free," applies here. Don't allow the government to assume total power. That will never work. Look at the examples of history. The Soviet Union was a human rights disaster. So are Cuba, North Korea, and China. It will be a disaster here, as well.

Chapter Six: Free Speech

If you give the government total power over our lives, dictating how we live and what we can say, then you allow the government to own you. Not as an analogy, but literally. If the government gets powerful enough, it will literally own everyone. We will just be numbers, and they will control how we live (but don't worry, that's not going to happen).

The conservatives recognize this potential end result and are fighting the liberals from achieving that outcome. From their perspective, and an accurate one, big government can only lead to bad outcomes. Ironically, the liberals still believe a good outcome is possible from big government. As I have pointed out, they are naïve. That outcome is impossible because the soul was not made to be controlled. It was made to be free.

When the soul leaves the human body after it dies, it finds itself completely free. The freedom and love that you will feel after you crossover to the spiritual planes is so joyous that you will feel like you have gone to Heaven. In fact, you will have simply gone home.

Humanity is trying to create Heaven on Earth, and it will succeed. In fact, you will begin to get a glimpse of that outcome toward the end of this decade, and more so in the middle of the next decade. You will begin to see how humanity is evolving. And trust me, the future has nothing in common with either the liberal or conservative agendas. A new way forward will emerge. A way forward where we begin to love one another and not control one another.

The conservatives want to control the lower and middle classes from upsetting the apple cart and breaking a system that works for them. The liberals want to break the system to build something that works for them. Both are clueless on how to create any meaningful change.

I'm writing this book to wake some of you up to the fact that both of those paths are dead ends, so that you can find the new way, the new path. I'm giving you the red pill of information.

Those still fighting for their side, either as a conservative or liberal, will hate these words. In fact, I will be vilified by both sides. But I have decided to share what I know to help humanity move forward. I already know the outcome, and know my words are not needed. But, on the other hand, as we each try to push humanity forward, we speed up that result.

I know this chapter was somewhat one-sided, with the liberals being the bad guys of censorship and anti-free speech. But the conservatives are nearly as bad at controlling narratives. There are many conservative media outlets and websites that attempt to control information that they release to the public. When you espouse false narratives (that we have the answers!), that is just as bad as censorship. Narratives are a way of controlling information. Censorship is only one side of the coin for free speech. Narratives are the other side.

Chapter Seven

Collectivism vs. Individualism

It's amazing that this topic is barely discussed by the MSM. *Fox News* mentions it occasionally, but it is completely ignored by the liberal media and liberal cable networks. I think we all know the definition of both, but I'll give a brief overview of each.

Collectivism is the idea or belief that the whole is more important than the individual. From a liberal orientation, it is the belief that the laws of society should be structured for the whole. Thus, when laws are proposed, the priority should be on how the law benefits the entirety of society, and not individuals or individual groups.

In theory, collectivism sounds logical. For instance, to implement laws that prevent discrimination, you have to focus on the entirety (the collective) of society. Moreover, if you want to control businesses from polluting, then focusing on all businesses and not a subset of individual businesses, is logical.

So, for some laws, focusing on the collective makes sense. The problem with collectivism is that it often goes too far and removes individual liberty. COVID-19 is an excellent example. The government used the idea of the collective as the basis for COVID-19 mandates. They thought that the government's response had to focus on the safety of the whole, and individual rights were a secondary concern.

In this type of scenario, it becomes the political philosophy of the administration in charge that dictates the approach. President Biden claimed that his mandates had nothing to do with freedom, and instead were about safety. Clearly, this was a political decision based on philosophical beliefs.

Did the Biden Administration even debate internally the potential impact of mandates on individual rights? I doubt it. That would be tantamount to questioning if they were making the right decision. It would also open the door to discussing what is considered misinformation. It opens up too many big questions. It's better to keep Pandora's box closed and see everything in black or white, with no gray. Thus, I'm sure the narrative was quickly decided that the focus had to be on the safety for ALL Americans. If some individuals wanted to take responsibility for their personal health, that was untenable and would not be allowed. This is why natural immunity from COVID was ignored from the beginning of the pandemic and continues to be ignored as the pandemic winds down.

At what point do individual rights become subsumed? Isn't that an important question? Can the government mandate vaccines to all citizens in the name of safety for the collective? Most liberals clearly say the answer is yes. Conversely, most conservatives hold the opposite belief. Consequently, it comes down to the courts to decide, and we had plenty of court cases regarding mandates during the pandemic.

As you can see, there is a serious divide of opinions and beliefs by both political parties over vaccine mandates. For the conservatives, the idea was my body, my choice. For the liberals, the idea was that the safety of the collective overrode individual rights.

What's scary about this event in American history was that it showed that liberals are willing to allow the government to dictate and decide what is best for the whole (the collective). Ironically, this was probably the best thing that could have happened to society. I'm not talking about COVID-19, but our reaction to it. Society became exposed to how easily our freedom can be removed. Biden said his mandates were not about freedom, but surely they were. If the government can stick a needle in your arm without your approval, that is a loss of freedom.

This event revealed that if we ignore the sanctity of personal freedom, it is a slippery slope that ends with the government becoming more powerful and steadily removing our individual freedoms. Before long, all citizens will be monitored 24/7 to protect the safety of the collective. This is already happening in China, and it is clearly occurring here to a certain extent. Edward Snowden told us all about the National Security Agency (NSA) data collection programs. Instead of being heralded as a whistleblower, he was demonized by the government and had to become a fugitive on the run. Why? Because he was a whistleblower of government secrets. How does that fit with a liberal mindset that the government is good? Are liberals okay with collecting information on all Americans that the NSA continues to do? The answer is yes, because they don't perceive individual rights as sacrosanct. In their view, it is the collective that is sacrosanct, and safety of the collective must come first.

If monitoring all citizens isn't dystopian enough for you, consider that in the future, a leftist-socialist government will probably collect the DNA of each child born and then decide their future. Freedom will be eliminated for many of these children. The government will decide how or if they can benefit society. This is already occurring in China, where children are identified for certain traits and then sent to schools that enhance these traits. Why? For the betterment of the collective.

We likely already have pre-crime programs today that utilize AI (artificial intelligence) to track those who are identified as a threat to society. If liberals have their way, these programs will proliferate for the good of the collective. Use your imagination on how this can be abused. We already have no-fly lists that have false positives. It's not a stretch to think that there will be many types of lists for those identified (perceived) to be breaking cultural norms.

If we continue down the road of focusing on the collective and ignoring individual rights, bad outcomes are surely to occur. It used to be that the worst thing that prevented you from getting a job was a felony conviction. In the future, your beliefs, behavior, and acquaintances could have the same impact.

So, collectivism is a philosophy with a slippery slope of bad outcomes. Sure, it sometimes makes sense to focus on the collective, but you should never ignore the sanctity of the individual. These individual freedoms need to be clearly designated in the Constitution, and the courts need to recognize these laws.

Individualism is the idea or belief that the individual is sovereign and sacrosanct. An individual's rights cannot be limited or encumbered as described by the Constitution and Bill of Rights. So, any collective law needs to take into account the rights given to individuals.

Liberals reading this book are asking, why are individual rights so important? The answer is that an individual has a soul. It is the soul that is important and needs to be respected. One of the reasons liberals reject individual rights is that they reject the idea of the soul. This rejection of the soul is a big reason why individualism is under attack today by both liberal politicians and their liberal supporters.

I don't think it is a coincidence that most conservatives today are Christians. They equate individual rights with their Christian values. They recognize the congruency between free will, freedom, and individual rights. Those beliefs all fit together and cannot be separated. In fact, they are all considered sacred values.

Chapter Seven: Collectivism vs. Individualism

Another belief of those who hold individualism as a sacred American value is the line in the Declaration of Independence that demands life, liberty, and the pursuit of happiness as inalienable rights. In other words, America was founded on the idea of individual freedom. That is what liberty and the pursuit of happiness imply.

From the Declaration of Independence, America was founded on the idea of a meritocracy, whereby the American Dream could be had through individual hard work. It also implied that the government would not impede this right of the people to pursue happiness.

Ironically, regardless of the Constitution and Declaration of Independence, liberals want to ignore this foundation of a meritocracy, and instead want to create a new version of America that is more collective-based and less individual-based. For instance, they want to remove grading and testing in schools. This is the epitome of a collectivist approach. Meritocracy-based societies create winners and losers, and liberals want to create more equity.

On a side note, liberals don't want society to debate the merits of this revolutionary reshaping of America. This is why they want to control information on the Internet. The more open the debate, the less likely society will agree to destroy our meritocracy. This is a major reason why conservatives have been banned from large social media sites. This is a big topic that they like to discuss.

The problem with individualism and a meritocracy is that you get inequity. The government then becomes the arbiter of how much unfairness is allowed, and how to rectify this lack of equality. That is where we are at today. We have the result of a meritocracy whereby a small minority of people have most of the wealth. The lower class and middle class get the scraps and are basically drowning in debt and working long hours to keep from going broke.

The liberals are simply tired of our meritocracy. It isn't working for the collective, so they want to try something different. They want to give more power to the government to remove individual rights and thereby create a society that works more fairly and equitably. Unfortunately, they will just make it worse by expanding the size and reach of government. Sadly, the woke mob is convinced this is the right solution and will fight this political cold war to the end.

Conversely, the conservatives and their embracement of individualism and meritocracy have rejected the importance of the collective. They reject that the collective can be kept in harmony and optimum efficiency by the government. Instead, they put the onus on individual responsibility. They reject that the collective needs to be under the control of the government. In fact, this type of government control is what they fight against.

The conservatives believe that it is not their responsibility to fix the problems of the collective. From their viewpoint, any attempt is some type of utopian pipedream that is impossible to accomplish. They believe that any attempt only leads to a dystopian future where freedom is removed, and prosperity is doomed.

The conservatives are correct: collectivists will create a dystopian society, whereby freedom is removed and limited. But what the conservatives miss is that their philosophy is just as flawed. The ideal of individualism and a meritocracy will lead to a similar dystopian outcome. While capitalism is acknowledged to have flaws, such as the manifestation of monopolies and the concentration of wealth, conservatism is not acknowledged to be flawed by conservatives.

Ironically, while conservatives ignore their flaws, liberals are quick to point them out. Individualism and meritocracy lead to winners and losers, where society is left with a preponderance of citizens who are struggling. These citizens who struggle end up

Chapter Seven: Collectivism vs. Individualism

breaking the laws that conservatives want enforced to maintain their quality of life. This is why liberals are defunding the police.

Liberals want life to be fairer in a country that is affluent. As conservatives deny that such a problem exists, society devolves into a state of dystopia. Such is life today. Crime is increasing, poverty is increasing, drug use is increasing, etc. Society is dying, yet conservatives look the other way and pretend it is not their fault.

While liberals don't have answers, neither do conservatives. In fact, they don't even want to try to find a solution. How can you find a solution to a problem that doesn't exist? From their perspective, if people would just take responsibility, the problems would fix themselves. So, conservatives point their fingers at the inner-city Democrats and blame them for the decay of society.

The liberals are trying to find a solution. This is why they are called progressives. The conservatives are not trying, and by not trying, they are failing. In fact, that failure is becoming obvious. It is the conservatives who have been in charge since 1980, when Reagan adopted globalism and put the current economic system in place. The political system hasn't changed much since 1980. Individualism and meritocracy are alive and well.

The 1980s and 1990s ushered in an era of affluence, with widespread consumer satisfaction. Products of every type were available. Every year new products came out. It was a consumer paradise. But it led us astray from the issues that create societal harmony. We lost sight of the fact that people were being left behind.

As the amazing explosion of new products and technology unfolded during that era, the middle class steadily decayed, and the lower class was left to fend for themselves. Globalism was expanding, and high-paying jobs were shifting overseas. The rust belt expanded to include multiple states, and small-town America was dying. This hollowing out of the middle class extended to the lower class. America was in decline and conservatives were in denial (they still are), and the liberal agenda was beginning to marinate.

Conservatives were euphoric during this era. They thought that meritocracy and individualism were working splendidly. They were in complete denial that the economic system was degrading. In fact, many of them are still in denial today!

Most conservatives believe that meritocracy and individualism work just fine and that all we need are a conservative Republican administration, low taxes, the rule of law, and limited government. A few tweaks to the economy, along with a Republican Congress, and all will be well. My main point here is that they have no ambition or intention of fixing the collective. This intransigence is what created the progressive movement and the move of the Democratic Party and MSM to the left. The liberal wing of America finally had enough.

This became apparent when Donald Trump became president in 2016. He was the trigger, but it didn't matter which Republican assumed office. Any conservative would have triggered the liberals. They were ready to be triggered. They had had enough of the conservative agenda, where the majority of Americans (and most of their constituents) were left behind. The America Dream had died and had become a lie.

How much crime and violence do we have to endure until a Republican speaks up and says this is our responsibility to fix? How much economic inequity and lack of opportunity do we have to endure before a Republican speaks up? Unfortunately, the answer is never, because they are afraid of the solutions. This is why this political cold war is so vitriolic.

Chapter Seven: Collectivism vs. Individualism

Both sides will fail because they can't see the solutions. If they looked at it from a spiritual perspective, it would be easy to see. They need to see that we are all connected, and all share the same consciousness. Then the liberal collectivists would see the importance of individual sovereignty. The conservatives would see the importance of economic opportunity and fairness.

Once you see the world through spiritual eyes, solutions become abundant and obvious. Both the liberals and conservatives will never have spiritual eyes because it is too much of a leap for their platforms and agendas. Instead, they will hang on to their philosophies until they disintegrate and fail. The solution is to leave these parties, stop voting, and look to those who have solutions. Unfortunately, these new solutions will be outside the mainstream. In fact, outside the political system.

You will feel like you are pulling away from society, but in fact, you will be creating a new society — a new era. The current one is busy dying. Well, that is a harsh word, I prefer *transitioning*. However, only a few Americans are currently transitioning and leading the way. Most Americans are either trying to hold on to the old way of life (conservatives) or fighting to create something new (liberals) within the current political system. Both don't have a future. This will soon become apparent, if it hasn't already.

Chapter Eight

THE PATH FORWARD

Most of you will not like this chapter. But as Tom Petty wrote, "It's wake-up time. Time to open up your eyes." I'm tempted to delay the release of this book until some of these ideas make their way into the public arena. However, if I feel compelled to write this book now. It's time.

Humanity is heading in a new direction, and the reason why is because it is rapidly evolving spiritually. This may not be apparent yet, but it will soon. I'm a metaphysical writer, and some of the ideas in this chapter will be new to you. I have already spoken about the idea that there is only one consciousness, of which we all share. This oneness of consciousness is the Creator (God), of which we are all a part. There is no separation between us and the Creator, nor from one another. What connects is consciousness.

This fundamental truth will now begin to spread throughout civilization. In fact, it is already spreading. It will underpin a new direction for humanity. A new question will begin to arise, how do we organize society to match this new understanding? First, many will recognize that the current system (political, cultural, social) is not going to work. So, people will stop voting, stop listening to politicians, and stop paying attention to the MSM.

That is the first step: pulling away. It has already begun on a small scale, but it will steadily increase as this decade progresses. People will begin forming small communities that are somewhat self-sustaining. The trend toward hyper-localization will have begun. These small communities will attempt to source what they need from within their local area. This will not be 100% practical, but for food, energy, and water it will be a priority for many of these communities.

The changes will be slow at first because the economy is not going to crash. It will muddle and linger, allowing people to hold onto their way of life, even if it continues to deteriorate. Many will hang on to their belief that society will return to normal, or at least some type of similar new normal. The political cold war will linger for many more years, as both sides attempt to acquire enough power to reshape America into their political ideology. Both political parties will be in denial that America is transforming into something completely different, even when it becomes obvious that the American era of global dominance is over. The political power that currently exists in Washington, D.C. will steadily evaporate, as it transfers to states and local communities.

At a certain point, Washington will lose its relevancy and will no longer have any sway on states and local communities. This won't happen for at least a decade and perhaps two. But it will become apparent at some point in the near future that this transition is underway.

It's easy to understand why Washington is going to lose its influence. One party (the Republicans) wants to continue the disenfranchisement of the lower class. The other party (the Democrats) wants to remake America into a socialist state, whereby freedom is severely restricted for both the citizens and businesses. Both ideologies are doomed to failure, especially at a time when spiritual awareness is expanding.

I think the Creator knew that the best way to create change was to create disharmony. And the more disharmony, the more potential for significant change. By creating two political parties with agendas that were not only in opposition to one another, but also completely misguided, the stage was set for a transition.

Chapter Eight: The Path Forward

To understand what we are transitioning to, you need to understand some spiritual concepts because this transition is spiritually directed. This will sound ludicrous to most of you, but this transition has been planned for thousands of years. The plan has always been to return this civilization to a state of harmony, where loves flourishes.

It was not known if we would succeed (without destroying ourselves), until around 2012. At that time, civilization's collective consciousness reached a level of spiritual awareness that was high enough (vibrationally) to evolve. The level of awareness has steadily increased since then and continues to expand (vibrationally) and evolve.

You may think this concept of a collective consciousness and spiritual awareness is ludicrous, but over the next 10 to 20 years, it will become apparent that it is not ludicrous, as love begins to flourish, and humanity goes in a new direction toward peace and harmony. The old souls, such as myself, will be wayshowers who lead the way. We have spiritual knowledge that humanity needs, and we will share it.

America is full of Christians. Perhaps as many as 75% of Americans consider themselves to be Christians. This is the group that is ripe to become spiritually aware. Only about 4% to 5% of Americans know without a doubt that they are a soul in a human body. This number is going to increase dramatically as Christians begin to realize that indeed they are a soul in a human body.

A big change for Christians will be that we are one with each other and one with the Creator (consciously). We indeed are all part of the Creator. We have to be, because nothing can exist that is separate from the Creator. Since this is true, we can drop the belief that the Devil wants our soul, or that the Creator is going to judge us, and perhaps send us to hell. That fear-based idea is going to be replaced with the idea that we are all eternal beings, and this is not our first lifetime.

The Christian idea that we were born in sin and this world is a place of good and evil, where the Devil tempts our soul, can be put to rest. It's fiction. The truth is that each human is an utterly amazing eternal soul that is one with God, one with the Creator, whatever term you want to use.

Humans need to realize their magnificence. That magnificence is not earned through deeds. It is true simply by existence. The existence of the soul, which is always magnificent. There is a saying that everyone learns who begins a spiritual journey: I AM. That saying means that your existence is all that matters. The fact that you have a consciousness is all that matters. That consciousness is forever. I AM. Say it out loud. You can't unlearn it. You just found out that you are eternal. Congratulations. You are equal to not just your fellow man, but with ALL souls. Do you now see why our political system is flawed and doomed to failure? Have your lucid eyes awoken?

This truth has been hidden from us because this planet has free will and has allowed humans to evolve on their own. Until the collective consciousness could raise its vibration high enough, the truth would remain hidden. The time has come for the truth to be released. Love is coming back to the planet. That will be the outcome of the truth being released.

Life is very simple if you can understand the basic truths. I've given you some already: there is only one consciousness, we are all connected, the Creator (God) encompasses the totality of consciousness, we are eternal, this is not our first incarnation, and the Creator gave us free will and does not judge.

Let me fill in the blanks of some other important basic truths. We are all evolving spiritually. All souls are here to learn. Learn what?

Chapter Eight: The Path Forward

Mostly, that love is our core, and that love is what is important. What makes this lesson so difficult in a human body is that we accept separation as a reality, when in fact, separation is a lie.

Once we accept separation, we are in denial of God. When we withhold unconditional love for another human being, we are denying God. This creates all kinds of traumas, and thus, learning experiences. We don't even realize that we are doing it most of the time. Instead of seeing another as a perfect embodiment of the Creator, we use ideas of who we think they are and how they should fit into our lives.

We judge others with conditional love to hold onto the idea of who we are. We are lying to them, and we are lying to ourselves, when the whole point of life is to find the truth. The only truth that exists is unconditional love. This is why the love of a mother for a child is so pure. The lesson for all of us is to hold that love for everyone. This, is where society is heading. You can get on that train now, later, or never. It's your choice, and there is no correct answer.

So, the acceptance of separation leads to a society based on lies, which are founded on ideas. All ideas are false unless they are based on the concept of one all-consuming integrated consciousness that has a foundation of unconditional love.

What I am writing in the chapter is not my opinion. This is the truth. Of course, everyone has their own version of the truth, and no two people can hold the same truth. This is why religions will now begin to wane. Each person has to find their own spirituality and truth within. Any dogma that people try to share with one another is only a trap.

So, while I call what I write in this chapter the truth, that is somewhat misleading. Most of the concepts are indeed true, but you will have to find that truth for yourself. That may seem somewhat contradictory, but spirituality is not something that is easily grasped. In fact, spiritual concepts cannot be taught with words. They must be experienced. But I digress.

These next two decades are going to be challenging for humanity. Families and friendships will be torn. Not because of war. Not because of economic collapse. But from spiritual ideas and spiritual concepts — what you are reading in this chapter.

Most of what you have read in this chapter probably sounds ludicrous. It's not, and it will become apparent this decade. The truth is about to be released to the masses. Humanity is just about ready. The lie of separation will not be a secret much longer.

As you drop your idea of separation, fear will be replaced by love. That is how love will manifest throughout the world and become the foundation of a new humanity. Steadily, love will begin to replace dissension and conflict that is so prevalent today. Then, as we learn to love ourselves and others, we will manifest harmony in both our lives and our communities. It's really that simple. Read that paragraph again.

To make a better world, you have to start with loving yourself. Not loving your ego-identity, but your soul-identity. This is not narcissism. This is healthy self-love for being one with the Creator and being an eternal soul. From that self-love, you are able to focus on taking care of your body and your health. This includes both your physical health and your mental (spiritual) health.

The world needs the best version of you. That should be your starting point. Once you create that, then all you have to do is be. Share your love: your love of self and your love of humanity. That is all that is needed. Period. Full Stop.

A healthy body shows respect for the soul and respect for the Creator, as well as humanity itself. A person who is in contact with their soul will always respect the body. Amazingly, self-love

Chapter Eight: The Path Forward

and a love of humanity is the most important thing to keep the body healthy. Why? Because love balances the body's (and soul's) energetic system.

Unfortunately, modern science still doesn't understand how soul energy balance is the key to good health. It will be a while until modern science understands that an energetic soul is intertwined with the body. But energetic healing will become more widely used in the near future.

So, love is not only how we manifest harmony in our lives and communities, it is also how we remain healthy. The future of humanity is a civilization based on love where harmony and health flourishes. Now, that will not manifest quickly, and will require a few generations. However, we get to be the generation that puts it in motion.

Unfortunately, the changes will be slow. Many of you who begin this transition will be frustrated at the slow pace of change. But that is how it has to be. We've already waited thousands of years, so what's a few more decades? The reward will be to know that we were part of the beginning and that we did our part. We will not be here to see the final outcome, but we will see change begin.

What do I mean by slow? Society will continue onward in its current form, while a small subset of people begin a transition into a new way of living. At first, it will be imperceptible, but then toward the end of this decade, the transition will become obvious to many.

While these new communities begin to form, society itself will be degrading. The large urban cities will continue to see the advance of more decay, more homelessness, and more crime. The suburban areas will begin to break down, with many people moving to safer areas with lower population densities.

There will be a palpable feeling that something is broken with society, and that it can't be fixed. There will be no return to normal. The political cold war will reach a crescendo as both sides continue to loathe one another. Red states and blue states will separate to such an extent that people will avoid travel to their political cold war adversaries.

The U.S. economy will muddle on, but with very little growth and a series of recessions that create significant hardship on non-affluent families. The federal government will no longer be able to use debt to stimulate the economy to grow. Without the luxury of a digital money printing press, we become analogous to a third-world economy, where growth becomes very sluggish.

Many corporations with household names will go out of business as the economy stagnates. Without a vibrant economy, America becomes hollowed out and ripe for change. The political cold war prevents any type of political solutions. And without a vibrant economy, it makes political solutions unviable. Although, even if they were viable, the political parties will be bereft of any ideas that could help.

Once the federal government becomes impotent for stimulating the economy, the transition into a new era will pick up speed. This will occur after the U.S. Government defaults on a portion of the debt owed on its U.S. Treasury bond obligations. At that time, the dollar will lose a significant amount of value. That is when the Fed will lose its ability to print at will. It will be the final blow to the U.S. economy and America's viability in its current form.

Fortunately, the U.S. economy will not collapse. The reason why is because of technology (especially the Internet), infrastructure, an established financial system, and contract law. These foundations will prevent the economy from imploding, but it will falter to a large degree. Not only will it falter, but it will not regain its prominence. The transition will be in motion.

Chapter Eight: The Path Forward

You will want to head West, although avoid the West Coast (California, Oregon, and Washington). There are fewer people West of the Mississippi. Fewer is better when things begin to unravel. Find a small town away from a big city. Grow and eat your own food. Drink clean water. Exercise and remain fit. Live simply. Focus on ways to help your local community. Get to know your neighbors. Get to know your community. This is how you create harmony and spread love. That is the path forward.

* * * *

This book has a conclusion as the final chapter, but I will include a brief summary here. If liberals win this political cold war, we will end up with a large tyrannical government that restricts freedom and dictates how we live our lives. If the conservatives win, we will end up with anarchy, as the middle class disappears and the lower class erupts into violence and crime.

Fortunately, neither side will win. Instead, society will steadily move away from both political parties and look for new answers. Those answers will be found in new spiritual truths that begin to spread throughout society. Those truths have not yet found their way into the mainstream, but will towards the end of this decade.

I've stated that many or most of the spiritual concepts that I have written about in this book would not be easy to accept. We are in the early innings of the spiritual shift. The idea that separation is a lie will not be accepted all at once. But it will be exposed to society soon, and for many of you, this is indeed your first exposure.

* * * *

Some of you will want to create a new political system for the new era. I have written a new constitution, which I have included in Appendix One. This will give you some ideas. It will work for a small community or a small country, perhaps up to ten million people; although, I think one million or less is ideal. This new constitution, and my explanation of it, is available on Amazon. The book title is *Post America: A New Constitution*.

* * * *

If you purchased this book on Amazon, I would appreciate it if you write a review. Reviews are essential for book sales.

Conclusion

SOME ADDED THOUGHTS

Because this is a controversial book, I did a pre-release and sent it to several people for feedback. Some of that feedback was added to the book, but most of it I will add here.

The feedback was interesting in that people see politics through their own biased lens. So, basically, both sides think they are right, just as I surmised in the preceding chapters. Republicans think they can fix our problems with their platform, and Democrats conversely think they can fix them, too. Clearly, both are in denial and refuse to acknowledge their weaknesses.

Moderate liberals were upset that I repeatedly used the term liberal (regardless of my stated liberal definition early on in the book) and lumped them together with extreme leftists. Many moderate liberals think they are the good guys and do not support some of the more radical ideas of the progressive socialists. But they are indeed supporting those positions when they vote Democrat.

The same goes with moderate Republicans. You can't vote Republican and deny that you are supporting the entire Republican platform, which is fighting against equity, equality, and opportunity for *all* Americans.

The liberals thought I was too easy on Trump, and that it showed that I was biased towards the conservatives. They wanted me to point out that Trump is a bigot, racist, and misogynist, with numerous accusations of sexual misconduct. The hatred of Trump is intense among liberals. They say it's his character, but I think it has more to do with his politics, and more to do with the political cold war in which we are currently embroiled.

Liberals were upset that I gave *Fox News* a free pass and didn't point out that all they do is spew lies. The liberals have a strong revulsion for *Fox News*. Conversely, the conservatives have the same strong revulsion for the MSM, and especially *CNN* and *MSNBC*.

The conservatives were upset that I didn't highlight the rampant crime in America and blame the Democrats for this outcome. They think America is imploding because of Democratic policies, especially with regard to law and order. I think this is a simplistic argument. The Republicans are just as guilty, which I think I pointed out in the book.

Liberals were apoplectic that I thought the 2020 election was possibly stolen, and that the *2000 Mules* documentary is fake. Well, if it is fake, then why didn't the January 6th Committee investigate it and prove it was fake? Instead, they simply called it fake without double-checking the evidence. The committee could have easily obtained the same cell phone data and disproved it.

Some said that I should have left out the spirituality and newage woo-woo. Well, that is the reason I wrote the book. I wanted readers to see where America is heading, and without understanding the looming spiritual shift, that was not possible.

Someone thought I was misleading when I stated that conservatives supported freedom. They said that the conservatives were the original cancel culture. They canceled women and would not allow them to vote. Much of that canceling was done during an earlier era. This book is focused from 1960 forward. But it is true that conservatives tend to question complete equality between men and women today. Plus, they are adept at canceling the LGBTQ movement. You could also argue that their antagonism against abortion restricts women's freedom.

Conclusion: Some Added Thoughts

* * * * *

I mentioned the middle class many times throughout the book, and I think it is a critical issue facing America today. In my opinion, neither party is focused on helping the middle class, even though it is what keeps America stable. Without a middle class and we will have anarchy, or no America at all.

I find it incredulous that we have allowed globalism to hollow out the middle class for the past 40 years. You have to be blind to not see that globalism is noxious to the middle class.

Very few politicians have highlighted this issue with any urgency. Trump did during his first presidential campaign, but it was all bluster and never brought any jobs back.

Here are three simple steps to bring the middle class back to life.

1) Require companies that import products into the U.S. to make a portion of those products here. We have one of the largest markets in the world. We should be leveraging that consumer buying power.

2) Consolidate the payscales for companies with more than 50 employees. This will create pay equity and fix the problem of the top 10% soaking up all the wealth.

3) Provide free online education for Grade 1 through college. And allow students to use any accredited online course towards a U.S. online college degree.

* * * * *

In closing, I want to point out the main differences between the parties, which are chasms that I don't think can be closed. I will do one paragraph for each one.

Abortion: Roe v. Wade is supposed to be overturned any day now. This is perhaps the most contentious issue. The conservatives are adamant that they are right and that abortion should be highly restricted. Conversely, liberals are adamant that restrictions should be limited, and all women should have control over their bodies. This battle will rage.

2nd Amendment: Liberals want to restrict access to guns, especially so-called assault weapons, which is a term that has an opaque definition. Conservatives are adamant that the 2nd Amendment should not be restricted. This battle will rage.

Freedom/Big Government: Both sides disagree with the reach of government and its impact on our lives. Liberals are more accommodating to the government's reach into our lives, which tends to restrict our freedom. This has become more pronounced as technology proliferates, and free speech and privacy issues have become more visible. Conversely, conservatives are dismayed with the expanded reach of government into our lives. This battle will rage.

Immigration: Liberals have been much more lax in recent years to close the border. Trump wanted to build a wall and was met with strong resistance from Congressional Democrats, who would not fund his plans. Under Biden, the border has been practically open. Once across, illegal immigrants have been given free bus rides by the U.S. Government. That would not have occurred under Trump. Ironically, the Republicans used to be lax on immigration in order to support big business, but in recent years they have turned more restrictive. This battle will rage.

Climate Change: This has become an issue that is growing in importance for liberals. They think the science has been proven. However, not so fast. Kryon (www.kryon.com) says that this is a cycle and was going to happen regardless of what humans did with carbon policies. Kryon says that it is going to get colder, which is the opposite of global warming. All of this carbon fear appears to be misguided. We should be afraid of a lack of food from cold temperatures. Ironically, once it started getting cold, scientists started blaming carbon for that as well. Conservatives tend to be skeptical of climate change and the need for a green revolution. This battle will rage.

Appendix One

A New Constitution

Preamble

We hold these truths to be self-evident, that all humans are created equal, that they are endowed by their Creator with certain unalienable Rights, which among these are Life, Liberty, Justice, and the Sovereignty of the soul. To secure these God-given rights, Governments are instituted among People, deriving their just powers from the consent of the governed.

Declaration

We the people, desire to form a country based on fairness, freedom, integrity, honor, justice, equality, and respect. The country will exist as a united whole that works together in harmony with cooperation. No one person or one group shall infringe upon the rights of others. Government shall remain limited in scope and size, with the citizens in charge of making all important decisions.

Guiding Principles

1. The liberty to be free without encumbrance.

2. Every human is a respected sovereign being with equal human rights.

3. Opportunity for everyone, and no one deprived of education and basic necessities.

4. Service to the country and not service to one's self.

5. If a person cries out for help, the country will come to their aid.

6. Crime will not be tolerated.

7. Government kept to a minimal level.

8. Thrive and enjoy life.

9. Reach for your dreams, but you may have to work hard to achieve them.

10. Respect the environment, which includes earth, water, air, and all life forms.

Country Values

We are all neighbors and should treat each other fairly and kindly. We are all equals and should consider the humanity of our actions. Helping one another should be a priority for everyone. Any injustice, unfairness, or discrimination will not be tolerated.

Business Philosophy

Our goal is sustainability over growth, stability over complexity, quality of life over achievement. While competition is required in a capitalistic system, conflict and competition do not have to overshadow our humanity.

Article I

Section 1

There will be no elected officials or elections. All government workers will be chosen from a selection pool using the profile web page of each citizen. Each citizen will be responsible for filling out their profile and maintaining it on the country's website. These profiles will include each citizen's education, work experience, and essays that include detailed information of their proficiencies. Each citizen can specify positions they would be interested in performing. They can volunteer for jobs or be assigned. Medical exemptions for government service will be available for the disabled.

A citizen's previous job position will be waiting for them after they return from public service. They can file a grievance with the arbitration panels if they have been discriminated against for missing time at work.

Article I

Section 2

Government positions will last at most one year, and after you have served, you will be excused for at least one year. Positions will be filled by selection committees comprised of currently serving government workers. These selection committees will be randomly generated based on existing similar positions.

There will be no individual leader of the country. Instead, there will be one group that defines the requirements needed by the country. This group will be comprised of four men and four women and will be called the board of directors, or the board. It will require the same vote from five board members to make a decision. All votes made by board members will be made public to the country on the day of a vote.

These ten positions will be chosen annually by a randomly selected committee of existing high-level government positions. This selection committee will attempt to find the best ten candidates from the country. Two of the chosen candidates will be designated as first and second alternates, who can stand in for board member absences. These alternates can also serve as alternates for selection committees and arbitration panels.

A member of the board, arbitration panel, or selection committee can be removed by an arbitration panel for unsuitable behavior. An arbitration decision in favor of a removal can be appealed twice. If a citizen is removed from one of these groups, they will be replaced by an alternate. A new alternate shall be found using the same method for finding alternates.

Article I

Section 3

There shall be no judges or juries. Instead, there shall only be arbitration panels comprised of citizens. The board of directors will have the authority to assign or delegate to other committees, the task of creating 1-year arbitration panels for all disputes, crimes, and misdemeanors. There can be several selection committees and several arbitration panels ... whatever the board of directors deems necessary.

Article I

Section 4

The board of directors has the authority to implement new laws, enter into trade agreements, and coin money. However, these laws and agreements can be re-written and changed by the succeeding board of directors. Moreover, the citizens can vote to overturn existing laws by a majority vote. There shall be no citizen voting to implement new laws, only to overturn existing laws.

Any decision made by the board that has an impact on the country must be codified into law so that citizens have the right to review these decisions and potentially overturn them.

If citizens overturn a law, the current board of directors cannot create a similar law in the same year. If they do so, a citizen can file a grievance to revoke the law, which will go to an arbitration panel.

Citizens can march and protest against any decision made by the board. Protests do not require a permit and can occur on public property. People can march on public roads, but not on public highways.

Article I

Section 5

Voting will occur on the 1st Tuesday in November if, during the year, 10% of the voter age population signs a petition to overturn an existing law. A majority vote is required to overturn a law. Digital signatures and digital voting are both acceptable. All citizens 21 years of age or older are eligible to vote. No voter registration is required.

All voting will be done using a secure immutable blockchain, and the results can be viewed by the public using a blockchain explorer. Voter identities will be concealed, although a voter will be able to see that their vote is on the blockchain and was counted.

Article I

Section 6

All arbitration decisions must be reached within 3 months of the filing. Decisions regarding disputes and crimes can be appealed twice. This can be considered a three strikes process. After three derogatory decisions, it is final. The appeals process must be completed within three years of the first arbitration decision. There is one exception to the three strikes process. If new evidence is discovered, it can be presented to the board of directors, which can reinitiate a new arbitration case. If the evidence is compelling, there is no statute of limitations.

All arbitration hearings are to be recorded and made available as part of the public record on the country's website.

Article I

Section 7

All selection committees and arbitration panels shall consist of four men and four women. If a member is absent, there will be alternates available. A majority vote will be used for decisions. The selection committee and arbitration panel members shall not use their religious or political beliefs for making government decisions. Instead, they will use the principles set forth in the constitution.

Article I

Section 8

Treaties, contracts, or laws with other countries must be approved by 70% of the electorate. These laws must be re-approved by 70% of the electorate every 10 years if they do not expire.

Article II

Section 1

Citizenship is a privilege and not a right. Each citizen is responsible for themselves and must hold the values of the country. While each citizen will be respected as a sovereign soul, this does not give them the right to disturb the harmony of the country.

Article II

Section 2

Instead of utilizing a series of laws, the country will rely on a single framework of what is unacceptable behavior. This will be called Disturbing the Harmony of the Country. This catch-all legal requirement will be implemented by the arbitration panels. While this may seem counter to the country's credo of fairness, arbitration panels will ensure it is not abused. The guiding principles of the country shall not be infringed.

Article II

Section 3

No standing army will exist or be organized. Local militias are allowed to form of their own accord, as long as their objective is for the defense and well-being of the country. The only long-term government employees will be police and firefighters. These assignments will last for five years, although citizens can be re-assigned to these positions on request by an existing police officer or firefighter.

Anyone suspected of violating a law or Disturbing the Harmony of the Country can be reported to the police, who will inform the arbitration panels.

Appendix One: A New Constitution

There shall be no secondary government police force or intelligence organizations. There shall be no sharing of personal information, except for those authorized to access medical records or validate a job applicant.

Article II

Section 4

All citizens will be included in the government database. This database will include the profile of each citizen. It will include their picture, retinal scan, address, phone number, email, height, weight, and eye color. It will also include their education level, work history, and additional proficiencies. The government will issue ID cards and passports based on this information, which will be free to obtain by each citizen. The data must be updated at least every five years. Employers will use the database to verify a citizen's identity. Anyone in the database is allowed to vote if they are 21 years of age.

Article II

Section 5

A citizen can lose their citizenship if they have been found guilty of disturbing the harmony of the country and have been declared banished. Arbitration boards have the authority to issue verdicts of either community service, fines, or banishment. If a citizen is banished, they will be given an escort to the border. If they come back, they will be banished to a remote location. (Article I, Section 6 allows a citizen to appeal an arbitration panel decision twice before the decision is final).

If a citizen or visitor is charged with disturbing the harmony of the country, they can be held by the police for a short duration while an arbitration panel makes a decision on either banishment, community service, or a fine. The maximum duration holding period will be 3 months.

Article III

Section 1

The department of revenue is responsible for collecting taxes. They are also responsible for issuing new money. The country's fiat currency shall be gold-backed and convertible into gold. Growth in the money supply shall be determined by the board of directors.

A country cryptocurrency will also be issued. Businesses will have the right to transact in the fiat or cryptocurrencies of their choice. Tax payments will be accepted in either the country's fiat currency or a specified cryptocurrency.

Article III

Section 2

Banks, insurance companies, and other finance companies shall all be nonprofit. There shall be no stock market, nor any publicly traded companies operating in the country. Only private businesses will be allowed to operate.

Crypto/blockchain DeFi (decentralized finance) shall be deemed legal. These companies can do commerce as finance companies. They will be required to be private nonprofit businesses. They can issue crypto tokens that trade on public exchanges.

Article III

Section 3

Businesses with more than 250 employees will use a maximum of 10 pay scales, whereby the top pay scale is no more than 10 times the lowest pay scale. If the business has fewer than 50 employees, then it is exempt. If it has fewer than 250 employees, then it will use a maximum of 7 pay scales, with the top pay scale no more than 7 times the lowest pay scale.

Any bonus pay or profit-sharing will be the exact same for all employees. If a business is sold, the profit is considered income for the owner. They do not have to share the profit with the employees. This creates incentives for people to start their own businesses. There are no limitations on how many businesses a citizen can own.

If a business is sold, if the business has any cash or assets, those transfer to the buyer. The owner of a business can only have an annual income of ten times (10x) the lowest paid employee. If the owner wants to assume ownership of any cash or assets of the company, they must give the employees equal amounts. If the owner gets $1,000, then each employee receives $1,000.

Article III

Section 4

Unions shall be illegal for both private and public employees. There shall be no collective bargaining. Any injustice, unfairness, or discrimination can be reported to the arbitration panels. Any business practices that are counter to the country's values can result in the loss of a business license.

Article III

Section 5

Inheritance and gifts shall be exempt from taxation and not treated as income. Transactions of services or personal property shall be exempt from taxation and not treated as income. Transactions of real-estate property shall be exempt from taxation, but any profit for the seller will be treated as income.

Article III

Section 6

A flat tax of 10% on all income will be imposed on all citizens. Businesses will be exempt from income tax. This tax will be due June 1st. It will be paid to the revenue department. This department will have the authority to assign investigators for irregular tax filings or late payments, which can be reported to the arbitration panels. The board of directors will have the authority to raise the income tax rate above 10%. However, citizens can vote to overturn this increase (refer to Article I, Section 4).

Article III

Section 7

A sales tax of 5% will be used for all transactions exchanging goods. There will be exemptions for food, medicine, medical treatment, medical equipment, and personal property. The board of directors will have the authority to raise the sales tax rate. However, the citizens can overturn this increase (refer to Article I, Section 4).

Article III

Section 8

There will be a 15% sales tax on overnight accommodations (room charges), gasoline, diesel, tobacco, alcohol, marijuana, sugar-flavored drinks, and fast food. The board of directors has the authority to add products to this list.

Article III

Section 9

An employee shall work a maximum of 30 hours per week for an employer, with overtime illegal. For those who want to work more hours, they can become a government volunteer, start a business, or work for more than one employer. Business owners and volunteers are exempt from this restriction.

Article III

Section 10

The minimum wage will be considered a living wage, and set by the board of directors annually on January 1st. Because the income of a business owner can only be 10x the lowest paid employee, the starting pay for many businesses will be higher than the minimum wage.

Article III

Section 11

Both a driver's license and vehicle registration will be free. No physical driver's license is required for driving. However, you must be 18 years old, pass an online test, and have an adult family member verify that you know how to drive. You can use your Government ID Card for identification. Vehicle registration can be done online, with the registration and license plate mailed to the citizen.

Article III

Section 12

If there is a budget deficit and additional revenue is necessary, the board of directors can raise the income tax rate, sales tax rate, fees, or implement tariffs. Any of these new laws can be overturned by a citizen vote (refer to Article I, Section 4).

The government will not incur debt or borrow money. Ideally, the government will have a large amount of surplus reserves. These reserves can be held in various assets, including fiat currency, gold bullion, silver bullion, and cryptocurrency.

If there is a trade deficit with another country, the recommended solution is to require that country to make (manufacture) a percentage of their product in our country.

Article III

Section 13

No toll roads will be allowed in the country. No cameras or electronic monitoring devices will be used to ticket vehicles for infractions on public roads or highways.

Article III

Section 14

Vehicle insurance will be handled by one private company and will be nonprofit. Their contract will be renewed every 3 years.

They will only insure damages to the vehicle or if the vehicle is stolen. The insurance company will be exempt from lawsuits. Citizens will be responsible for negligent driving and can be fined by arbitration panels or given community service. Driving privileges can also be suspended or revoked.

Article III

Section 15

The owner of a property without a mortgage or lien shall not be evicted from his property unless an arbitration panel rules in favor of his/her banishment from the country. In the event of banishment, the offender will be paid the current market rate for their property.

A property owner or renter can be evicted from their place of residence by an arbitration panel if a grievance was filed from the lack of payment on a mortgage, lien, or rent.

Article III

Section 16

Citizens are encouraged to have their own gardens and grow their own food. They are allowed to sell their food at local farmer's markets or in front of their homes. These home-grown products will be considered to be personal property and not subject to income tax.

Article III

Section 17

If a company grows in size to the point that it is in a dominant position and prevents competition, the board has the power to split the company into two separate companies. If companies are found to collude for the purpose of both companies increasing their profits, they can be found to be disrupting the harmony of the community. The result can be fines, the firing of employees, and other judgments from an arbitration panel.

If a company is found to be disrupting the harmony of the community, it is recommended that management and the owner(s) are replaced, if this is a viable solution for the arbitration panel to select.

Article III

Section 18

All government income will come from income taxes, sales taxes, fees, and tariffs. This means that there will be no property tax. If you own your house or business, it is truly yours. You own the ground underneath it.

Article IV

Section 1

No country currency or cryptocurrency shall be given to those in need by the government. Instead, assistance will be given directly to those in need. Public housing centers, public food centers, public healthcare centers, and public job training centers will be supported by the government. Free transportation to these centers will be available to the public.

Article IV

Section 2

Public housing centers will be separated into different groupings, such as the short-term homeless, long-term homeless, disabled, mentally ill, and elderly. With the availability of public housing, there will be no need for sleeping on the streets. While some citizens may prefer this lifestyle, it will be required for them to sleep at the public housing centers if they are homeless.

Article IV

Section 3

The public housing centers for short-term homeless will be designed to provide a temporary refuge and not a permanent community. It will only provide the bare necessities and not attempt to create a high quality of life or sustainable living arrangements. The food menu will be austere and the amenities just as austere. Conversely, it should provide free counseling, job training, and job placement. Those residing in these centers should be given help to get back on their feet.

Article IV

Section 4

Any house that has not been lived in for 12 months must be put on the market for sale or sold at auction. Any house on the market for more than 6 months must be sold at auction. All houses offered at auction must have an open house (minimum of 2 hours) for 3 days prior to the auction. All houses up for auction will be sold at the highest bid without a minimum price.

Article IV

Section 5

Single-family houses must not be owned for rental income. All existing single-family rentals must be sold or put up for auction within 6 months after the constitution is approved. The value of all single-family houses will be appraised when the constitution is approved. From that point forward, they can only appreciate in value as determined by arbitration panels. If you want to sell your house, an arbitration panel will determine its price.

Article IV

Section 6

Multi-unit housing will be allowed as rental properties, although they must be nonprofit. All multi-unit housing rental rates will be determined annually by arbitration panels, based on the financial situation of the owner and the current market rates. If an owner sells a multi-unit housing property, the profit will be considered income.

It's possible for a private business to own more than one multi-unit housing complex. However, owners of multi-unit housing will not be allowed to become enriched by charging high rent. The rental rates paid by tenants will be based on the financial health of the owners. If the owners have no debt on the property, then rates can be lowered.

Article IV

Section 7

Healthcare shall be a three-tier system. The first tier will be private healthcare using licensed professionals. The second tier will be private healthcare using holistic practitioners. The third tier will be the public option, where healthcare (all doctors, dentists, optometrists, etc.) is a single-payer system run by the country. Citizens are only charged what they can afford, with a maximum of 3% of their income for the calendar year.

All healthcare-related businesses shall be nonprofit. Doctors' salaries can be a maximum of 10 times the lowest salary in the organization. Fees charged to patients will be subject to review by arbitration panels for potential excessive charges, which can be requested by patients. Health and nutrition shall be taught in high school for at least a single year. The focus of this education will be on preventing disease and staying healthy.

Article IV

Section 8

Medical doctors shall require a medical license, whereas holistic practitioners shall be self-regulated. Pharmaceutical drugs and health supplements shall be self-regulated. However, any citizen can submit a complaint to the arbitration panels to ban a drug or supplement. A country website to share information about local medical doctors, holistic practitioners, pharmaceutical drugs, and supplements shall be created and open to the public for posting information.

Article IV

Section 9

Vaccinations shall be optional and not mandated. Employers and schools cannot mandate vaccinations. No entity in the country can mandate a vaccination.

Article IV

Section 10

Water provided to communities will be tested annually, with the results released to the public. Citizens can submit complaints if the water is not considered satisfactory. Arbitration panels can request improvements to water quality.

Article IV

Section 11

The economy will attempt to be circular, whereby re-usage is supported with the goal of sustainability. This means recycling and re-usage; solar and wind power; new energy generation technology; and sustainable farming will all be supported with tax breaks.

Article IV

Section 12

Farmland can only be owned by a farmer who is using the land for farming. It cannot be owned for investment income or as an investment. The most farmland an individual or company can own is 10,000 acres. If farmland is not utilized for a 3-year period, then it must be sold prior to the end of the 3-year period or put up for public auction.

Article IV

Section 13

Appendix One: A New Constitution

The government cannot own land unless that land is needed for government buildings. The government cannot own any businesses or have an interest any private business enterprise, even if it is a non-profit. There must be a distinct divide between government entities and private entities.

Article IV

Section 14

If a corporation gets fined more than $25 million by the government for breaking the law, then the CEO is fired without receiving any further compensation (including their pension or any promised future compensation). They cannot return to work for that company for 5 years. Plus, the CEO is potentially liable for a personal fine, as well as being exposed to potential legal actions stemming from the misdeed. As a citizen, the CEO can appeal all legal decisions up to three times.

Article V

Section 1

The postal service, cable service, garbage service, phone service, water service, sewer service, maintenance of roads and bridges, electrical service, and natural gas service will be private and awarded to the lowest bidder every 3 years. The board of directors can add services to this list if it is in the interest of the country.

Article V

Section 2

Anyone is allowed to visit the country. There are no border guards or immigration officials. No passports or visas are required to visit. Visitors who want to stay for longer than one year must find employment, in which case they will be given a work visa. Visitors who do not find employment must leave after one year.

Hotels, multi-unit rentals, and citizens are required to report country visitors of more than 30 days.

Anyone found to be a visitor who has extended their visit beyond one year will be banished immediately. These violations will be treated seriously by the country because there will be many people who want to live in a utopian environment. Violators will lose their opportunity for a return visit and placed in a database. No business will be allowed to hire anyone in this database. Plus, anyone abetting a violator will be significantly fined.

Businesses are allowed to hire non-citizens to come and work. These non-citizens will be given work visas, and their immediate family can come with them. Any non-citizens found working without a work visa will be banished. Knowingly hiring a non-citizen without a work visa is illegal. If a non-citizen works in the country for five years, they can request citizenship. Their time worked does not have to be continuous.

Non-citizens can start and own their own businesses. If a non-citizen starts a new business, they must submit their financial records for the first five years. If the business is not generating sufficient revenue, then it can be at risk of losing its business license. If this occurs, then the visitor will have to leave the country.

Article V

Section 3

There are few business regulations other than following the country's building codes and honoring the principles of the country. A business license is free and can be obtained online. There are no reporting requirements, although financial statements must be kept for 10 years in the event of an audit. A business owner found to be in violation of maintaining financial records can lose their privilege to hold a business license.

Article V

Section 4

All food products sold in retail stores must have labels that include the ingredients. No GMO products can be grown or sold in the country. No pharmaceutical drugs can be given to animals intended for food production unless administered by a veterinarian for an illness. No herbicides or other harmful chemicals can be used within the country near food production. The board of directors can use its discretion to create additional laws that protect the public's health and safety.

All products sold must be labeled, except for personal property, which is exempt. The labeling requirements are defined by the board.

Article V

Section 5

Morality will not be determined by statutes in the constitution. Morality will be the responsibility of parents and adults. Gun laws, illicit drug laws, gambling laws, and other morality-based laws will be determined by the board and not the constitution.

Local communities can protest the existence or non-existence of morality-based laws. If a local community wants to allow or disallow morality-based laws, they can petition the board to implement them. A community must show an overwhelming support or lack of support for the board to add or remove a morality-based law.

Article V

Section 6

No smoking ordinances at indoor or outdoor public places or workplaces shall be allowed. Public parks are exempt, as well as where people live, which is considered to be personal private spaces. A personal private space can only be entered by the police with a probable cause warrant.

Article V

Section 7

Any form of advertising to enact or overturn laws is illegal. Any form of advertising that undermines the country's harmony is illegal.

Article V

Section 8

All public schools will have an armed security guard and a single point of entry with a metal detector. All public schools will have cameras and be monitored remotely for potential gun violence. Those who are offsite monitoring the school cameras and the onsite security guard will have a reliable communication channel.

Article V

Section 9

No one can possess a gun until the age of 25, unless hunting with their parent's or relative's gun. Those caught in possession of a gun prior to the age of 25 face a 5-year sentence. Those caught helping someone under the age of 25 obtain possession of a gun face a 3-year sentence.

Article VI

Section 1

Education shall be the highest priority of the country. Children will get the opportunity for a high-quality education. Teachers and principals will be reviewed annually for performance. Poor performance reviews will lead to terminations.

Article VI

Section 2

Education will be free for students from pre-school through college. Each school will provide daycare for any student in need.

Schools will not be public institutions. Instead, they will be run by nonprofit private companies, with three-year contracts.

Article VI

Section 3

Students and parents can choose which school to attend. There will be an online option for students who choose to study from home. They can switch schools at any time. However, problem students can be relegated to specific schools (and potentially online schools) to ensure high-quality education for all.

Article VI

Section 4

Students must pass an exam at the 6th grade and 8th grade level to move forward. They must also pass an exam to graduate from high school to become eligible for a college education.

Any student who fails their exam at the 6th grade or 8th grade level, can attend summer school and attempt to pass the test. If they do not pass, then they must repeat that grade level. Those who fail their high school graduation exam can attend summer school and retake the test.

Article VI

Section 5

The option for free college education will mostly be performed online, with face-to-face educational settings used out of necessity.

Article VII

Section 1

All public land, when the constitution is approved, will transfer to the country's ownership. Private businesses can make requests to obtain public land for development. Arbitration panels will approve or deny and set the selling price for the parcel of land.

All private land that is not developed will transfer to the country's ownership. Before this transfer of ownership occurs, the private owners can make a request to develop the land into an operating business within 3 years. They can also sell the land if they can find a party who will develop the land within 3 years.

Article VII

Section 2

All water rights and minerals rights will be owned by the country. Private businesses can request leases for mining or access to water. Arbitration panels will determine the annual fees and renewal periods for these leases.

Article VII

Section 3

No licenses will be required for hunting and fishing. Hunting and fishing seasons and rules will be determined annually by the board of directors. Hunting and fishing areas will be included in their announcement, which will be posted on the country's website.

Article VII

Section 4

Public parks and community cleanliness will be maintained by both government employees and volunteers. Arbitration panels can also assign community service to offenders of disturbing the country's harmony to help with these duties.

The board of directors can assign community service to teenagers if the country requires help with cleaning up a public area.

Bill of Rights: Amendments

Amendment 1

Freedom will not be impinged without the guiding principles of the constitution taken into consideration.

Amendment 2

Spirituality and religion will be a personal matter and not infringed or discriminated against. However, if a religion is deemed counter to the guiding principles of the constitution, it will be banned.

Amendment 3

Freedom of speech and a free press will be protected to the extent that it is not discriminatory or slanderous. All opinions are protected.

Amendment 4

Citizens and visitors will not be held without a charge. All will have a hearing by an arbitration panel in a timely manner (maximum of 3 months). There shall not be a death penalty.

Amendment 5

No citizen or visitor will be subject to unlawful searches or seizures. A person's possessions, be they things, records, or ideas, shall not be taken without due process of an arbitration panel. A person's physical and mental health shall be protected.

Amendment 6

Any form of discrimination is deemed illegal. Impacted parties can seek compensation from arbitration panels.

Amendment 7

Whistleblowers who report infractions will be protected. No citizen or visitor will be compelled to be a witness or provide information in a legal matter.

Amendment 8

All citizens have the right to file a grievance against a citizen, business, or government function. This shall be heard by an arbitration panel in a timely manner (within 3 months). If the grievance is identified as a frivolous complaint, the arbitration panel has the authority to side against the plaintiff.

Amendment 9

Citizens can collect signatures from one-third of the electorate for a referendum to modify the constitution. These signatures can be collected electronically. A two-thirds electorate vote is required to pass the referendum.

Amendment 10

There shall be one national holiday each month. On these holidays, no one shall work except the following: hospital staff, police and fire departments, and travel-related industries. The board of directors can modify this list as needed

Appendix Two

MICHAEL TEACHINGS

Soul Stages

Infant: which is the first stage, we learn survival lessons.

Baby: we learn how to follow directions and how to assimilate into a group.

Young: we learn lessons of the ego, where we become preoccupied with our own identity.

Mature: we learn lessons about our emotions. Here, relationships are paramount, and traumas and dramas are common.

Old: which is the last stage, we learn lessons about spirituality and unconditional love. This results in spiritual enlightenment.

Seven Levels

There are seven levels in each stage. We begin at the infant stage at level one and then progress from there. It usually requires at least one lifetime to progress to the next level. It is not uncommon for souls to get stuck and spend many lifetimes at one level. Note that we do not regress.

Seven Roles

Server: oriented toward helping others.
Priest: oriented toward spiritual issues.
Artisan: oriented toward creating things.
Sage: oriented toward entertaining others.
Warrior: oriented toward accomplishing.
King: oriented toward ruling.
Scholar: oriented toward learning.

Note: We can choose a combination of these if we desire.

Read my two books, *Conversations With an Immortal* and *Spirit Club* for more understanding of the Michael Teachings.

www.ingramcontent.com/pod-product-compliance
Lightning Source LLC
LaVergne TN
LVHW021827060526
838201LV00058B/3547